LIBERTY IN THE MODERN STATE

BY THE SAME AUTHOR

THE AMERICAN DEMOCRACY

FAITH, REASON, AND CIVILIZATION

REFLECTIONS ON THE REVOLUTION OF OUR TIME

WHERE DO WE GO FROM HERE?

THE AMERICAN PRESIDENCY

THE DANGER OF BEING A GENTLEMAN AND OTHER ESSAYS

PARLIAMENTARY GOVERNMENT IN ENGLAND

THE STATE IN THEORY AND PRACTICE

A GRAMMAR OF POLITICS

THE FOUNDATIONS OF SOVEREIGNTY AND OTHER ESSAYS

STUDIES IN LAW AND POLITICS

AN INTRODUCTION TO POLITICS

DEMOCRACY IN CRISIS

THE RISE OF EUROPEAN LIBERALISM

KARL MARX

THE SOCIALIST TRADITION IN THE FRENCH REVOLUTION

AUTHORITY IN THE MODERN STATE

THE PROBLEM OF SOVEREIGNTY

POLITICAL THOUGHT IN ENGLAND FROM LOCKE TO BENTHAM

COMMUNISM

THE DANGERS OF OBEDIENCE AND OTHER ESSAYS

LIBERTY
in the Modern State

BY HAROLD J. LASKI

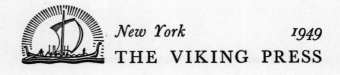
New York   *1949*
THE VIKING PRESS

TO LÉON AND JANOT

WHO FOUGHT SO NOBLY FOR LIBERTY.

WITH DEEP AFFECTION AND RESPECT

H. J. L.

PREFACE
TO THE EDITION OF 1949

IN this new edition I have made very considerable changes both in the introduction and in the original text; after ten years so momentous as those since 1937, I hope that I have learned something which makes the perspective of the central principles in this book more fully adapted to the experience through which we have passed. In the reconstruction of the text, I should like to acknowledge how much I have learned from long discussions in war-time with my colleagues, Mr. H. L. Beales, Dr. W. A. Lewis, Dr. O. Kahn-Freund, and Mr. A. Radomsysler. I owe much, also, to my friend Professor Perry Miller, of Harvard University, whom the American Army was good enough to send to London, so that, in the intervals of his military work, I could benefit by his imaginative insight and his remarkable learning. I alone, of course, have the responsibility for the weaknesses of the book.

The dedication is to two of the bravest fighters for freedom it has been my good fortune to know. To have won their friendship is one of the great experiences of my life.

H. J. L.

August 28th, 1947.
The London School of Economics
and Political Science.

PREFACE
TO THE EDITION OF 1930

IN the summer of 1929 I was invited to give the Colver lectures
at Brown University; I was honoured by being able to accept.
But my appointment, a few months later, as a member of the
Lord Chancellor's Committee on Delegated Legislation compelled me to withdraw from the post. I have thought, however,
that the publication of the lectures (a condition of their delivery)
might not be inopportune at the present time.

The book must speak for itself. Here I would only acknowledge the debt it owes to many of my friends, and especially to the
late Mr. Justice Holmes, the late Professor L. T. Hobhouse,
Mr. R. H. Tawney, and Professor (now Mr. Justice) Felix Frankfurter. It owes much, too, to my seminar at the London School
of Economic and Political Science, the members of which have
dissected it almost word by word. I need not say that none of
these has any responsibility for the opinions I have expressed.

H. J. L.

Jan. 1st, 1930.
The London School of Economics
and Political Science.

CONTENTS

LIBERTY IN THE MODERN STATE

INTRODUCTION

1

THIS book was written in 1930. When it was reprinted in 1937, I added to it an introduction in which I gave what seemed to me compelling reason for the view that the safeguards of liberty had visibly deteriorated all over the world. Since then, a second world war has been fought, against the Fascist nations and their satellites. Alike in Europe and the Far East, it resulted in the unconditional surrender of the Fascists. Many of their most prominent leaders have been hanged or committed suicide; others have been sentenced to long terms of imprisonment. Out of the ashes of the League of Nations there has arisen the United Nations organization, dedicated, like its predecessor, to the preservation of peace and the general improvement of man's lot in every land; this time, moreover, membership in the United Nations, with all its obligations, has been accepted by the United States of America and by Soviet Russia, each of which has been given a seat on the vital executive body of the new institution—the Security Council.

An immense victory has been won over those dark forces which, between the two world wars, everywhere threatened the survival of democracy and freedom. I do not, nevertheless, believe that any honest observer would truthfully say that the future of liberty is beyond all hazard. If we assume that the future of liberty depends upon the realization of those four freedoms upon which President Roosevelt laid such eloquent emphasis, there is little reason to feel any certainty that the future of liberty is secure. Grave economic crisis over most of the world makes freedom from want an

ideal that is bound to remain an empty one for long years to come.
There can be no freedom from fear while international rivalry
is so tense, above all when one, though only one, of the new
weapons that may be used if that rivalry is allowed to drift to war
is the atomic bomb. If it is an exaggeration to say that there is
less freedom of expression than there was between the war of 1914
and the war of 1939, it is certainly true to say that the status of free
expression is still in the danger zone over very wide areas; in
particular, the discovery of atomic fission, and of similar weapons
of mass destruction, has struck a blow at free expression in what
was once the international community of science from which there
is very little prospect of recovery unless and until there is a recovery
of international security substantially different in quality from
anything we have known since 1914. A good deal of the right to
freedom of worship has been restored; but, except in Moslem and
Roman Catholic countries, this seems more the result of a declin-
ing interest in religion, a growth of what may be fairly called
a nihilism in the realm of values, than of a positive attainment of
a faith by which men of goodwill everywhere feel themselves
bound.

The years of war, no less than the years in which, if there has
not been peace, at least there has been a lull in the open conflict
of states, have thrown a clear light upon the conditions in which
alone liberty can be regarded as safe. Liberty needs an expanding
economy as its primary condition; for where this obtains, men feel
that they have hope, and hope is, perhaps, the most vital condition
for the respect of law. Where a society has an expanding economy
men feel a sense of spaciousness, the existence of opportunity, the
chance of going forward. There is an atmosphere of exhilaration,
a readiness for adventure, a conviction that private advancement
is genuinely related to public welfare. Such a society has confidence
in itself. It does not see threat in doubt, it is prepared to draw
widely the boundaries of discussion.

It is when the economy of a society begins to contract that liberty
is in danger. Economic contractions always mean fear, and fear

always breeds suspicion. It is then that the rulers of a society begin to regard liberty with dislike. They know that people are no longer at ease, that they are doubtful about the wisdom of their governors, that they begin to listen to new voices, that they are likely to demand changes. What could be endured in an expanding economy as discomfort begins to make itself felt as grievance. Expectation grows that the government will remedy the grievance. It may ask to do so; but it can succeed only if it discovers the way forward to new conditions of economic expansion. It may well fail to do so; and, if it fails, there are only two methods by which it may hope to maintain its authority. The one is internal repression, and the other is external war.

Neither, obviously enough, can, in its nature, be other than an attack upon liberty. What internal repression may mean, at its worst, we saw in Hitlerite Germany during the war; there millions were callously assassinated by methods incompatible even with the lowest levels of civilized living, and the rulers of Germany held down practically the whole German population by a calculated system of terror. Germany, indeed, was only the worst example of government by barbarism. Its example was infectious and spread with grim swiftness to all of its satellites, as, also, to its Eastern partner, Japan. Nor must one fail to note the grave legacy left by these habits. Not, perhaps, since the seventeenth century, have men been either more careless about the infliction of unnecessary pain, or more deaf to appeals for mercy, than they have been in the years since the surrender of Japan in August 1945. As I write, there appears in the London *Times* [1] an appeal for aid on behalf of the ten million victims of cholera in China, victims whose plight is, for the most part, the outcome of hostilities in the last two years. We know that a great deal of Greece is still on the verge of starvation. We know that, alike in victorious Russia and in defeated Germany, there are millions who still have insufficient food and clothing and shelter. We can, indeed, go further, and say that, in the United States, richer today than any country has ever

1 August 22, 1947.

been in history, some proportion of its citizens between one-fourth and one-third live on the very margins of adequacy.

All of us are well aware that conditions such as these make it difficult to give to liberty that full place in the lives of mankind which is one of the great ends for which this war was fought. All of us, moreover, are well aware that the idea of liberty is differently conceived in different countries. Americans insist that no one can enjoy liberty; the denial of "free enterprise" is incompatible with the achievement of liberty. In Great Britain, the idea of liberty generally denies the Russian outlook, on the one hand, and the American on the other. There are countries, Egypt, for example, or Saudi Arabia, where a very small ruling class means by liberty the maintenance of its own power and wealth, and has no sort of interest in extending the benefits of liberty to the great mass of the peoples; it is, indeed, almost true to say that, in both Egypt and Saudi Arabia, outside a narrow circle of privileged people, ordinary men and women have no more idea of freedom than did most of the slaves of ancient Greece or Rome. Their lives are conditioned to a poverty so profound that the thing of which, overwhelmingly, they are compelled to think is how they can satisfy the primary impulses to gain food and shelter. The idea of liberty, as it is debated by social philosophers, involves discussion of experience and concepts far too complex ever to have entered into their lives. The observer can easily be led to report that they are wholly indifferent to it, and that an attempt to arouse them from their present inertia would involve an unreasonable effort. And yet, over large parts of Germany today, the observer would note a similar inertia among millions of citizens. He would be compelled to remark that they, too, were so absorbed in the sheer effort to live that the moral values associated with liberty had faded from their minds. But, on reflection, he would be bound to remember that, even under Hitler, to many of these millions, those moral values had been felt as something it was urgent to preserve, even to extend, and that only the destruction caused by catastrophic defeat had obliterated their significance from innumerable German minds.

The war, in fact, has merely served to re-emphasize certain truths about liberty which are almost as old as civilization itself. An interest in liberty begins when men have ceased to be overwhelmed by the problem of sheer existence; when they have a chance of leisure, the opportunity to reflect upon their situation, in a degree which, if small, is nevertheless real, to recognize that they need not helplessly accept the routine in which, before, they seemed hopelessly immersed. Economic sufficiency and leisure for thought—these are the primary conditions for the free man. But economic sufficiency, as this war has shown, comes when the productive capacity of a society is so organized that the free man has continuous access to these two conditions. The organization of productive capacity involves certain economic relations between men. And the validity of those relations depends on whether they make possible that access to ways of increased production which makes, in its turn, for the kind of distribution conferring immediate satisfaction and the right to hope that increasing satisfaction may be expected. We have seen systems of such relations in the past which have waxed and waned in terms of their ability to satisfy these criteria. We have seen systems of ideas develop to defend or to attack relationships in which men felt their vital interests were involved. And what has become obvious is that, at critical points, this attack or defence gives rise to emotions so passionate among men on either side, that circumstances may make it impossible for them any longer to reason with one another, and, as in France in 1789, or in Russia in 1917, men fight it out with one another until one side has won the mastery of state power in the community.

Into this highly abstract framework, we can fit, without an undue straining of the facts, the contemporary situation. In most countries of the present time, it has become impossible to satisfy demand without exacting from the masses who live by the sale of their labour-power alone sacrifices they are not prepared to make. Most of them, accordingly, have been driven to some kind of planned economy in order, not merely to preserve social peace, but to improve the productive capacity at their disposal. That planning means the use of the state power to direct the energies of men in one direction rather than another. It limits, accordingly, one kind of free enterprise, in which production is determined merely by the impersonal mechanism of the market. It was found that dependence upon the market economy meant a perpetual succession of booms and slumps in which what counted for most was not the needs of the community as a whole, but the wants of those who, whether as individual citizens within a nation, or as nations within the international community, were in a position to make the most effective demands upon the market economy. The day has passed when, over most of the world, the major instruments of production at least could be left in private hands. Where they were so left, the danger developed rapidly that the unequal claim to well-being would mean mass unemployment, and that this, in its turn, would beget disastrous social tensions which it was beyond the power of society to resolve by constitutional means. When tensions of this kind can be settled only by "violence," it is plain that freedom is certain to be suspended.

Nothing of this is seriously disturbed by the fact that the majority of Americans still cling to the system they call "free enterprise." For until the outbreak of the Second World War the United States also was in the grip of mass unemployment; and it had averted disaster only by immense programmes of public works and public relief by which it had restricted the unfettered play of the market economy. The war, moreover, as it developed, became increasingly for Americans a gigantic programme of public works. They achieved what was virtually full employment partly because millions of them entered the armed forces, and millions more were engaged in providing the material required to make possible the victory of those armed forces. When the war ended, the United States was in a quite special position. Alone among the major powers engaged in war, its productive capacity was not merely unimpaired, but even increased; and alone among them, also, it was in a position to supply a large proportion of the demands for goods and services that it encountered. Yet, quite obviously, that

Introduction

was, at least contingently, a temporary position. Demands from foreign nations could be effective only in so far as these nations were able to pay for what they required; and they could pay for them only if they were able, directly or indirectly, to sell to the United States enough of their own products to balance their purchases, or to export gold in place of their products. The only alternative open was that the United States should lend to any foreign nation in difficulty enough purchasing power to enable it to continue to buy American products until, as it was hoped, the economy of that nation would be sufficiently reconstituted to enable it to buy them without assistance of this kind. For if the purchase of American goods were to cease, there would, obviously, be unemployment in the United States; in a market economy it is broadly true that what is produced must be sold profitably in order to continue the process of production. If the foreign customers of the United States were unable to purchase its commodities, its export trade would shrink, and there would at once be unemployment in American industries dependent upon export. At that stage, there would be three possibilities open to the government of the United States. It might so reorganize the purchasing power of its own citizens as to enable them to possess an "effective" demand equal, or approximately so, to the loss of its foreign trade. It might make new loans in the hope that these would buy time with which the foreigner could rebuild his independent power to purchase. Or it might force its goods into foreign markets by selling them at prices so far below the cost of their production that it would be compelled to use public funds to subsidize the manufacturers and merchants who lived by their power to sell them at a profit.

The first of these three methods would mean the abandonment of a "free market" by the United States, and the adoption of some form of planned economy instead. The second could succeed only if the conditions on which the new loans were made did effectively restore the economy of those nations which accepted them. The third would, inevitably, have the result of so disorganizing the domestic market into which American goods were forced, that

the nation concerned would be driven to safeguard its own producers by limiting or prohibiting altogether the entry of American goods. That would, in its turn, involve countermeasures on
the part of the American government to defend the interests of
its own producers. This might ultimately develop into economic
war; and there is, of course, the danger that the economic war
might involve interests so profound that it would become, first,
a threat to security, and then, out of the feelings born of insecurity, into actual war itself. At every stage of such an evolution
as this, it is clear that the liberty of a social order would be cast
into jeopardy.

We live in a world where the interrelation of nations is so close
that a situation of this kind is bound to weaken the foundations
of any civilization which seeks to make the four freedoms of which
President Roosevelt spoke a normal part of its daily life. For once
a major power, whether it be the United States or Soviet Russia,
uses its might to enforce acceptance of the system to which it
regards itself as committed, it is bound to mobilize on its side all
those, either among its own citizens or among citizens in foreign
states, who believe they will be advantaged by its policy, and thus
to sharpen the internal cleavages and external conflicts between
nations. National and international unity begin to degenerate.
The proponents on both sides begin to take steps to strengthen the
principles of their policy and to weaken that of their opponents.
Each side may well proclaim that it has no interest save peace. It
may advance arguments to prove that only by means of its policy
can justice or liberty or the common well-being of nations be
secured. It is essential for us to understand that all this, even when
those who expound it are convinced of its truth, is above everything propaganda, intended to put the best face possible on the
case for a given policy. That emerges with striking clarity in the
denial by the United States that there is any freedom behind the
"iron curtain" which, as it holds, Russia has erected against any
objective scrutiny of its internal life and, to a lesser extent, that of
the peoples who look to Russia for leadership. Not less confidently

does Russia deny that there is any "real" freedom in the United States and in the countries which come within its sphere of influence.

The effort of the nineteenth century to separate economics from politics has plainly broken down. As early as the eighties of the last century, a German officer had said to Engels that "the basis of warfare is primarily the economic life of peoples"; [2] and no serious observer now doubts that this is the case. The strength of a people lies in the skill with which it can, in the last resort, mobilize its economic resources and its public opinion in the service of its political objectives; and, at the present stage of civilization, it is still true, however regrettably, that war is the final arbiter between different political objectives. Since the character of political objectives in any given community depends upon the possession of the state power, it follows logically that it is necessary to possess it in order to change the character of any political objective.

Here lies the central weakness in the approach we make to the problem of liberty. "Modern liberalism," wrote Leonard Hobhouse,[3] "postulates not that there is an actually existing harmony requiring nothing but prudence and judgment for its effective operation, but only that there is a possible ethical harmony to which . . . men might attain." But here, obviously, Hobhouse is abandoning the theme and the purpose of classical liberalism, which argued quite precisely that, given "prudence and judgment," the impersonal mechanism of the market of itself achieved social justice. Once there is introduced into this functioning an "ethical" strain, it is at once admitted that there is no "harmony of interests" in society without interfering with the market economy. This at once involves the need to admit the duty of interference by the state power on behalf of that harmony of interests deemed most desirable by the community. In a political democracy based, as it must be based, on representative institutions, the character of the duty to interfere must be determined by the party or parties

---

2 Friedrich Engels, *Anti-Dühring* (Leipzig: 1878), p. 196.
3 *Liberalism* (London: Williams and Norgate, 1911), p. 129.

which possess a majority in the legislative assembly of the society. Implied in this basis is that parties are sufficiently at one upon fundamentals so that they can agree to differ peacefully on matters within the framework those fundamentals define.

It is no use our evading the issue that there can be no liberty once agreement upon fundamentals has broken down; and it is obvious that over wide areas of the world it has already broken down, and that in such areas government by persuasion has had to give way to government by force. But once force is called into play, it must have some operative end it seeks to attain; and it is bound to compel those who dissent from that end either to accept it or to be punished for their dissent. And since every government must try to commend the end which it seeks both on rational and emotional grounds, it is bound to mobilize in its support all the agencies it can organize, and to deprive those hostile to it, so far as possible, of the means of organization. That is why there has evolved since 1917, and ever more intensely since 1945, the one-party state. The depth of the compulsions it exercises is essentially the measure of disagreement that it cannot overcome. The one-party state means, literally, what it is called. For all effective purposes, the state power becomes the apparatus of the party, so that the party can use the supreme coercive power to make its will into law. It is thus able not only to enforce unity on the society, but also to repress those who oppose the unity of the society by putting them in a position where they are bound to break the law. In this atmosphere criticism passes easily into conspiracy, and the attempt by a group within the party to capture its control is bound, if it fails, to be something it is difficult to separate from treason. Since the one-party state excludes, by definition, the right to open opposition, it is inevitable that the critics of the regime should be driven underground. But this means that the state power is always conscious of being faced by a secret danger; and it is to guard against this that the government—which is the party—is driven to organize, and, in no small part, to depend upon, a secret police. This, in its turn, is bound to provoke an atmosphere of suspicion; for not only does a secret police, by its very nature, put each citizen on guard against his neighbour, but it gives envious or jealous men the opportunity to use its power to wreak vengeance upon those by whom they believe themselves to be wronged.

The one-party state is under the constant temptation to overpass the boundaries beyond which government degenerates into dictatorship. And it remains in our own day, as it was when Thucydides described the revolutionary struggle among the Corcyreans, that, in these conditions, the rulers use words without relation to their meaning, so that servile obedience is hailed as freedom and the unity imposed by compulsion is heralded as the fulfilment of democracy. What is so dangerous in habits of this kind is that they grow by what they feed on, that, also, they are infectious, and that if, in high crisis, they are defended as a grim necessity by honourable men, they are exploited when crisis is absent by the sadists, the sycophants, the men with a lust for power for its own sake. The one-party system has as its supreme defect the fact that men must either give their consciences into the party's keeping or be regarded as capable of treason, if they desire to be active in political life. For while it is unquestionably true that there are many subjects, especially of technical and administrative detail, on which the rulers in a one-party state encourage criticism and discussion, all fundamental initiative there comes from above, and not from below; and there is no instance known to me in which a change in the personnel in the small oligarchy of those who hold the keys of the state power is not determined from within itself as something the outcome of which not merely the mass of citizens, but even the members of the party itself, must passively accept. This is as true of the leadership of the Russian Communist party today as it was of the Jacobins during the French Revolution. The critical mind is at a discount where, as in societies of this kind, the one-party system necessarily generates what Mr. and Mrs. Webb have fairly termed the "disease of orthodoxy."

I should myself fully admit that societies built like Soviet Russia upon the one-party system may be definitely progressive and eager to secure the well-being of their citizens. But I should argue that their decision to achieve progress by coercion and not by persuasion is bound to put the fulfilment of liberty at a grave disadvantage. It makes too many people look outside themselves for the course of action and for ideas. It replaces individuality by a collective man, whose notions of good and bad, wisdom and unwisdom, even the beautiful and the ugly, are ceaselessly conditioned by the methods of mass propaganda. No people can argue on its knees; and no one who examines the fantastic adulation which is lavished upon Generalissimo Stalin can doubt that it is a form of idolatry which is bound to subdue the ordinary man. Canonization ought to follow death, and not precede it; contemporaries who seek to anticipate the verdict of history in such a fashion only succeed in putting the social mind in fetters. And the longer progress is forced upon society, the more men are conditioned to a situation where they lose the habit of realizing that it is a civic obligation to think for themselves and that there are always circumstances in which they have no moral alternative but to make known the truth they see, however uncomfortable, with all their power.

I do not argue for one moment that a two-party, still less a multi-party state, is necessarily a guarantee of freedom. That always depends, first, on the economic forces in a society, and, second, on their relation to its political structure. It is clear, for example, that the two-party system in such capitalist democracies as Great Britain and the United States has been compatible with the deliberate use of the state power against the masses, even where there is universal suffrage. No one who has watched the hysterical witch-hunts against "radicals" all over the United States since 1945, and remembers the emphatic insistence with which the Declaration of Independence affirms the "inalienable" right of a people to change the character of its government, can argue that universal suffrage alone is any assurance that, even under its auspices, a people will get the government it desires or secure from the members of that government the measures to which they are pledged. Some of the statutes repugnant to freedom which have been passed and applied in the states of the American federal union are so drawn that almost any utterance might be penalized if the accused were brought before a biased judge.[4] It is, indeed, difficult in any capitalist country for a person of known radical views to obtain fair treatment in the courts, even where there is no obvious atmosphere of danger. And a Socialist government which, even with a majority, takes office in a capitalist society the institutions of which are formally democratic cannot help but be aware of the fairly narrow limits within which it may successfully manœuvre, and the danger to which it is exposed if it embarks upon measures which disturb the "confidence" of men of property.

There is, in truth, no real shadow of doubt that it is upon the issue of property that the whole problem of liberty hinges today, as it has always done in the past. There is a point, never capable of exact definition, up to which the men of property are willing to buy off the opponents of capitalism by measures of social reform. But when that point is reached, there is always the gravest danger that men of property, if they have to make their choice between their possessions and democratic institutions, will prefer their possessions and will destroy democratic institutions. That was the history of constitutional monarchy in Italy after the rise of fascism, and of the Weimar Republic even before the rise of Hitlerism; Hitler, indeed, rose to power essentially because it became obvious to the men who ruled Krupp and I. G. Farben that he was the instrument they desired. The breaking-point is not an intra-national one merely. The victorious Allies put the reactionary Horthy regime in power in Hungary in 1919 because they feared communism; and the government of the United States in 1947 aids anti-communist regimes like those of Greece and Turkey, and refuses assistance to states which, like Poland and Czechoslovakia, are on friendly terms with Soviet Russia, by exactly the same logic. It was to make certain that property was secure in Europe after 1917

---

[4] See the formidable list of them in Zechariah Chafee, *Free Speech in the United States* (Cambridge: Harvard University Press, 1941), p. 575.

that the Lloyd George government, with the enthusiastic support
of Mr. Winston Churchill, helped any sorry adventurer it could
find to make war upon the Bolsheviks. It is tin that rules Bolivia;
and at least two of the Latin American republics live or die by the
goodwill of the United Fruit Company of the United States. Even
a Labour government in Great Britain has not hesitated to break
its often and solemnly pledged word to the Jews about immigration into Palestine in order to make sure of its hold upon the oil
of the Middle East; and, to that end, it has even been willing not
only to go through the tragi-comedy of king-making in Trans-
jordania, to maintain the goodwill of a small class of functionless
effendi to whom the purposes of socialism are devoid even of
meaning, but also to act in Palestine as its worst Tory predecessors
acted in Ireland and in India. The lesson has still to be learned
that purposes which can be enforced only by military power have
rarely had the endurance to outlive the ideas to which they are
opposed.

It is almost a century since de Tocqueville, on the eve of the
annus mirabilis which gave to the working class its first full
sense of international solidarity, warned the French Chamber of
Deputies that the political question had become a social question. It is this transformation which has given a new context
to every one of the historic freedoms and made the general issue
of liberty so much more intricate than at any previous time. That
is true of freedom of the person; it is not easy to see how any
government situated like that of Great Britain in 1940 could have
done without the power of preventive detention. It is true of
freedom of speech and of freedom of the press; state ownership, as
in Russia, private ownership, as in most Western European countries, group ownership, as in Czechoslovakia, none of them gives
the results we require. Freedom of association obviously halts
when it enables either a Fascist leader to recruit his army of gang-
sters, or American industrial corporations to employ hired thugs
to prevent the growth of trade unionism among their workers. Nor
is it easy, in principle, to defend any claim to religious freedom if

some particular church seeks to obtain from the state power special privileges which give to its members what is in fact a priority denied to those outside its communion. We are all agreed, in principle, that freedom from want is desirable; but it is obvious enough from the discussions over the establishment of the international Food and Agricultural Organization, that none of the primary food-producing states is willing to give to such an institution the executive authority necessary to make it effective. They prefer the colourless neutrality of a fact-finding committee, even though, as Sir John Boyd Orr has said, we cannot feed a starving people on statistical tables. We all desire freedom from fear: but there is no community organized as a state that has yet been willing to surrender its sovereignty in order to aid in the creation of conditions which alone make possible the banishment of fear.

Looking back over the years since 1914, as that epoch is set in its historic context, I think there are two conclusions which are inevitable. The first is that private ownership of the means of production is no longer compatible with democratic institutions, and that, accordingly, the more prolonged its continuance, the more certain it is to result in problems which are unlikely to be settled by peaceful means. Though the tradition of constitutionalism is deeply rooted both in Great Britain and in the United States, I should not except either of them from this conclusion. The impact of two world wars upon Great Britain has made necessary revolutionary changes in its economy, and they will have to be made with a swiftness for which the propertied class is probably not psychologically prepared. I do not share the general faith in the British "genius for compromise"; that was, I believe, the outcome of a special set of historical circumstances that are not likely to be repeated. It has, moreover, still to be shown whether a Labour government will measure up to the demands of not merely one crisis, but a series of crises, which will test every ounce its members have of courage and determination and the power to choose the men proportionate to the tasks it faces; and two years' experience of government has shown that it has not yet learned

the elementary lesson that the more it encourages Socialist states
abroad the more likely it is to maintain its socialism at home.
Foreign policy must directly reflect domestic purpose if it is to be
successful; it must reach through form to substance if it is not to
be the expression of capitalist aims decked out in new tropes of
rhetoric. The United States, with all its immense productive
power, is further even than Great Britain from solving the problem
of a rational distribution of wealth, because its political structure
is so much less mature than its economic, and because there are
endemic in its life certain forms of corruption and violence which
are incompatible with the method of constitutional persuasion;
to this, I think, must be added that the hate produced among men
of property by Franklin Roosevelt's very moderate social reforms
is a danger signal that no serious observer is entitled to neglect.

The second conclusion is, in my own view, the supreme imperative of the next century, and we disobey its clear implications at
our peril. We have entered upon an epoch in which it is daily
more clear that the principle of national sovereignty has exhausted
its usefulness. Certain functions of government are so clearly international in character that we cannot rely upon the co-operation
of so-called "independent and equal" sovereign states to achieve
the cosmopolitan lawmaking that has become essential. It is not
only that the "independence and equality" of states is a juristic
fiction with no roots in political reality; it is a harmful fiction
because it obscures the reality to which we need to pay attention.
I do not pretend to foresee the stages by which we shall transcend
the national state; nor do I deny that national feeling is still a deep
passion, to which adequate institutional respect must be paid. I
can argue only that the more fully we separate the concepts of
nation and state, and get clear in our own minds the area of activity
over which each can legitimately range, the more fully we shall
understand the issue before us. And, in my own judgment, little is
gained, at the present time, by thinking in terms of territorial
federation—of a United States of Europe, of a Federated Western
Europe, and so forth. It is, in any case, increasingly doubtful

whether territorial federalism is not now obsolete; [5] and it is at least probable that no constitution could be worked out with either the essential flexibility in the division of powers, or the necessary avoidance of the complexities inherent in judicial review.

The way to conditions which make liberty possible seems to me to lie through the kind of functional federalism of which, thus far, the Tennessee Valley Authority has been the outstanding example. It is through supra-national planning in fields like electric power or transport, or an integrated economy of coal and steel, that we can best hope to attain this end. It is, of course, impossible to leave such planning in private hands; and, within safeguards approved by the United Nations, it is essential to give the authorities charged with the application of such plans the effective governmental authority to implement them. A similar type of planning for food has been, as I have noted, proposed by Sir John Orr, and I have no sort of doubt that were this to become effective the gain would be immeasurable. Liberty, and therefore civilization, we must remember, is still a matter of the existence of an adequate food supply, equitably distributed; and this we have not yet attained in the history of the world. We shall not attain it while the nation-state exists as the basic unit of political organization, for the simple reason that, in most countries, the capitalist character of the state power still makes it an instrument for subordinating the well-being of the many to the prior legal claims of the few. Our present level of education enables those who shape the purpose of the state to evoke in its support a national feeling which may be perverted to ends in fact in complete contradiction to what are objectively the interests of the nation. It is only if we are able to organize in time loyalties alternative to those which the state exacts that we can hope to achieve the conditions where men can hope for freedom.

If we can organize in time: that is the vital issue upon which

[5] Cf. my article "The Obsolescence of Federalism," in the *New Republic*, May, 3, 1939; and Gordon Greenwood, *The Future of Australian Federalism* (Melbourne: Melbourne University Press, 1946), an important book with a valuable bibliography.

turn all the issues of freedom. Nineteen twenty-nine was not one of
the passing cyclical crises which capitalism in the previous hundred years had been able so easily to transcend. It must be remembered that, seven years after the great depression, no nation had
achieved its 1929 level of production; and those which had sur-
passed it in 1939, most notably Germany and Japan, had done so
because their whole economy had been based upon preparation
for war. One stage of the conflict for which they had made ready
is over. But a new phase has begun in which the United States,
more quickly than it is agreeable to realize, must either win full
employment by drastic redistribution of wealth within its own
territories, or export its unemployment with catastrophic results
to the rest of the world. There is, indeed, the middle way of what
the Germans call *Wehrwirtschaft* (a war economy), but that is,
once more, incompatible with liberty, since it necessarily involves
militarization on an enormous scale—and it is obvious that the
American mind would, today, be wholly averse to the ideology of
militarism. It is, indeed, possible that, in the United States as
elsewhere, the technological implications of modern warfare may
make possible a new type of militarism unrecognizable to those
who look for its historic characteristics; of fourteen million men
mobilized by the United States in the Second World War, Army
and Marine infantry numbered less than one and a half million.[6]
Anyone who thinks for one moment of the effort involved in
building the atomic bomb will not find it difficult to realize that,
in the new warfare, the engineering factory is a unit of the army,
and the worker may be in uniform without being aware of it.
The new militarism may clothe itself in civilian uniform; and, if
the present relations of production are maintained, it may be imposed upon a people who see in its development no more than a
way to full employment. That can only strengthen the tendencies
—already so great—to monopoly capitalism; and it is still more
true of the great corporations today than it was when General

[6] Cf. General Marshall's report: *The Winning of the War in Europe and the
Pacific* (Washington: 1946), p. 119.

Négrier wrote of them nearly forty years ago that *"les sociétés financières estiment que les gouvernements ont le devoir de faire la guerre pour assurer leurs bénéfices."* [7]

Anyone to whom liberty is the root of civilized living can see that the dangers which threaten it are part of a world crisis in which time is no longer on our side. We are moving steadily to a new catastrophe. We can see its causes; we are aware of the remedies by which it may be met and withstood. Our tragedy is that the character of our social thinking is still set by the categories of nineteenth-century speculation, particularly in the economic realm; while our technological development leaps forward so swiftly that the gap between technology and thought grows ever more wide. We have reached the point where liberty depends upon revolutionary reforms; it is the ultimate foundation of our way of life that we have to change. It is time to say with all the urgency we can muster that the alternative to change is a new dark age in which even the memory of freedom may be forgotten in the bitter struggle to survive.

2

This is the danger that confronts us in our time; and there is no answer to that danger save the courage to organize against it while there is time. I say the courage to organize against it; for in our day not less than in that of Pericles the secret of all liberty remains courage. We acquiesce in the loss of freedom every time we are silent in the face of injustice. The more we insist that it is not our concern, the easier we make the demagogue's task. For it is of the essence of liberty that it should depend for its maintenance upon the respect it can arouse in humble men. Their power to maintain it lies in their willingness to organize themselves for its maintenance. It has no foe more subtle than their sense of apathy or helplessness. And men who have known what liberty

[7] "The corporations believe that it is the government's duty to make war so that they may be assured of their profits." Cited in Edouard Dolléans, *Histoire du Mouvement Ouvrier* (Paris: A. Colin, 1939), Vol. XVII, p. 151.

means will not surrender it if they are awakened to the danger
it faces. Their weakness lies in their inability to penetrate beneath
the mask its enemies assume. They have been habituated to obedience. They have not been schooled to read the lesson of the historic
movement. The economic interdependence of the world, the necessary relation of boom and slump in capitalism, that system's re-
quirement of an army of unemployed, the degree to which methods
of production must shape the forms of the political system to the
requirements of their own immanent logic, these things are not
the staple intellectual diet upon which they are fed. Most of them
are born to live and die without a glimpse of any of the forces by
which the world is moved. They have to judge its governance only
as they faintly descry the larger context in which its own vast
secular changes impinge on their petty lives. Before them is the
daily need to live, the exacting toil of work, the need for play and
sleep and a brief hour of love. They are schooled to obedience
by the rigorous discipline of their lives. It is no easy task to give
them the sense of grave dangers to be arrested, of big ideas which
need an army to fight for them. Only great leadership can strike
their imagination into that action which responds to the call.

The first necessity of that leadership is recognition of the situation we occupy. It is not enough to know that we live in dangerous days; it is above all urgent to recognize the nature of the
danger. It is not enough, either, to insist upon the insecurity of the
times; it is fundamental to recognize the nature of the insecurity.
Our danger and our insecurity are no different in their ultimate
causation from the danger and the insecurity which brought about
the collapse of Greek and Roman civilizations. We have come to
the end of an economic system exactly as they came to an end.
Our relations of production contradict the forces of production
exactly now as then. What distinguishes our position from that of
our predecessors is the greater knowledge we have of the dynamics
of social change. We are able, as the Greeks and Romans were not,
to become the masters of our social destiny if we so will. The
means of a new and fuller security lie at our disposal, and, with

its advent, the means, also, of a new and fuller liberty. For what has characterized our liberty in the past, in almost every significant field, has been its limitation by the implications of the economic system under which we have lived. Liberty for us has been always hindered and hampered by its necessary subordination to the claims of property. It has been enjoyed only as its exercise has not threatened the owners of economic power. Now that the consequences of their ownership once more endanger the foundations of civilization, they seek to abandon liberty that they may preserve their privileges. If we permit its abandonment, at some stage conflict is certain. For the mind of man cannot, in the long run, be habituated to tyranny; at some stage the slave revolts against his master.

They seek to abandon liberty; and they will succeed unless we organize ourselves to prevent their success.

I do not for one moment underestimate the risks or the difficulties of the task. To transform the ultimate economic foundations of society is the most hazardous enterprise to which men can lay their hands. It touches habits more profound, prejudices and convictions more sincerely held, than any other form of social change. It can never be effected without the pain and disappointment that invariably accompany the failure of established expectations. Perhaps, even, it cannot be accomplished save at the price of violent conflict between man and man.

The alternatives before us are stark. Either we must acquiesce in the maintenance of an economic system which, day by day, brought, as it may bring again, war and fascism as its inevitable price, or we must seek to change the system. There is no remedy now for our ills save, with all its intricate complexities, the planned production of our economic resources for community consumption. This means—let us face the fact—that private ownership of the means of production must go. With it must go, too, the class structure of society, with all the privileges it has annexed to the system of ownership it has maintained. It is possible, though I do not think it likely, that if we organize for this end in time, we may persuade men, because the initiative that comes with the possession of state power is in our hands, peacefully to acquiesce in this transformation. Certainly if we are successful in that persuasion we shall have accomplished the most beneficent revolution in the history of the human race. It is, on the other hand, possible that the privileged will fight rather than give way. In that event, because we are organized, there is at least the chance of victory. Acquiescence, in any case, is only a postponement of conflict. To organize the unity of those who seek the new social order is, at the worst, to give them a fighting chance.

And it cannot be too strongly emphasized that those who seek the new social order are in this hour soldiers in the army of freedom. They alone can end the exploitation of man by man. They only have it in their power to establish a society in which there is recognized to be either an equal claim upon the common good or differences in return only to claims rationally justified by their ability to augment the sum of the common good. Our present economic system cannot display these characteristics. "The reward," said John Stuart Mill of its working, "instead of being proportioned to the labour and abstinence of the individual, is almost in an inverse ratio to it; those who receive the least labour and abstain the most." A society like ours can be secure only as its foundations permit of its continuous expansions; it is now decisively clear that the age of its expansion is ended. With its contraction, it is unable to satisfy progressively the wants of men, and it is therefore deemed, by all excluded from its privileges, an irrational and unjust society. As such, it is incapable of that security which, as this book has argued, is the basic condition of freedom.

Not only so. The greater the effort to restore its security upon its present foundations, the greater the attack upon freedom that is involved. For the way to that restoration lies through the suppression of all the instrumentalities of freedom. Its method is depicted for us by the experience of the Fascist countries; they achieved security by transforming their societies into prisons.

Science and art were there no longer free creations of the human mind; they were the instruments of the authority that coerces men into obedience. To seek security, people were compelled to deny their own cultural heritage; and a new and more terrible inquisition presided over the thoughts of men. Yet they did not achieve security even at the terrible price they sought to pay for it. For not only, in the very shadow of the prison-house itself, did brave men and women arise to challenge its authority—Matteotti and Roselli in Italy, Dimitrov and Thälmann in Germany; but it could not meet the challenge all social systems have to meet—the need so to develop its resources peacefully that it could progressively advance the standard of its people's life. In the long run—though, indeed, the run may be very long—war and circuses are no substitute for bread and the free life of the human spirit. Men in the end come to recognize this, and, when the recognition dawns, they renew their courage to shake off their chains.

That, let us add in conclusion, is the essential truth behind the grim struggle in the Soviet Union. It has been part of the strategy of the enemies of freedom in part to decry the accomplishment of the Soviet Union's makers, and in part to declare that the price is too heavy for the end. It is vital for those who care for freedom to maintain a proper perspective in this matter. The Soviet Union has been the pioneer of a new civilization. The conditions upon which it began the task of its building were of a magnitude unexampled in our experience. Its leaders came to power in a country accustomed only to bloody tyranny, racked and impoverished by unsuccessful war. Its peoples were overwhelmingly illiterate and untrained in the use of that industrial technology upon which the standards of modern civilization depend. Its task of construction was begun amidst civil war, intervention from without, famine, and pestilence. For the first years of the regime's existence the people lived quite literally in a state of siege. The leaders could not have coped with the gigantic problems they confronted unless they had governed in terms suitable to a state of siege. They were insecure in the two fundamental senses that they had to overcome the resistance of powerful internal enemies, often munitioned from without, and that they lived in constant danger of attack from foreign states. No doubt Lenin and his colleagues were responsible, in the first seven years of the Revolution, for blunders, mistakes, even crimes. It is nevertheless true that, in those years, they accomplished a remarkable work of renovation. They accomplished it, moreover, in such a fashion that, within ten years of the overthrow of the Czar, they were able to proceed to the full socialization of the productive system. In the last decade, the achievements have been immense. The war has been won; unemployment has been abolished; illiteracy has been conquered; the growing productivity of the Soviet Union stands in startling contrast to the deliberate organization of scarcity in capitalist states. In the treatment of criminals, in the scientific handling of backward peoples, in the application of science to industry and agriculture, in the democratization of culture, in the conquest of racial prejudice, and in the provision of opportunity to the individual—in the full sense the career opened to the talents—the Soviet Union stands today in the forefront of civilization. It is, of course, true that, judged by the standards of Great Britain or the United States, its material levels of life are low; it has not rivalled in twenty years the unimpeded century-long development of the most progressive capitalist states. The true comparison, of course, is with pre-revolutionary Russia; and the gains, both material and spiritual, are immense. In wages, hours of labour, conditions of sanitation and safety, industrial security, and educational opportunity, the comparison is at every point favourable to the new regime.

But the Soviet Union remains, after thirty years, definitely a dictatorship; and this has, naturally enough, caused grief and disappointment to men all over the world who care for freedom. Not only is it a dictatorship, but the ruthlessness with which it has suppressed those hostile to its authority has been sombrely seen in the grim tale of executions since the assassination of Kirov, and in the deep suspicion with which it regards not only the

manœuvres of its enemies, but a good deal of the devotion of its
friends. In the classic sense the Four Freedoms do not exist in the
Soviet Union. There is no liberty to criticize the fundamentals of
the regime. There is no liberty to found parties to oust the Communist leaders. A man cannot found a journal of opinion or
publish a book or hold a meeting to advocate views which, in
the judgment of the dictatorship, would threaten the stability of
the system. A citizen who sought to overthrow the philosophy of
Marx, or to urge that Trotsky, and not Stalin, wore the true
mantle of Lenin's tradition, would soon find himself on the way
to exile or imprisonment. There are bureaucratic stupidities like
the denial of passports to the Russian-born wives of British air-
men. There are diplomatic blunders like that which suggests a
declaration, about as fertile as the Kellogg Pact, to help in the area
of atomic energy. Art, the drama, music, the cinema—through
all of these the dictatorship has sought to pour a stream of tendency, often with ludicrous, and sometimes with tragic, results.

To see the Soviet dictatorship in a proper perspective, certain
things must be borne in mind. In the first place, with all its faults,
it is wholly different in character from that of Mussolini or Hitler.
Wide as are the differences in the rewards it confers, there is no
evidence of the reappearance of a class that lives by owning; and
it remains broadly true that differences in those rewards are related
to the individual's contribution to the sum of social welfare. It
is, moreover, the case that the purpose of the dictatorship is meas-
urably and directly related to that welfare; the standard of living
increasingly rose before 1941, and, granted peace, will rise again;
the regime is built upon the principle of planned production for
community consumption. It must, further, be remembered that
the whole effort of the Soviet Union has been conducted through-
out in an atmosphere of contingent or actual war. If there has been
little doubt of its internal stability since 1924, there has been constant reason, especially since 1933, to fear foreign attack; and the
evidence goes only too plainly to show that its foreign enemies
counted upon, and even sought to stimulate, internal dissension

and weakness, as the basis of that attack. And this must be set in
the context of a people whose memories of the civil wars are vivid,
who have been taught by their experience to find groups with
doctrinal differences arming themselves for ruthless conflict. They
are aware that the basic principle of their social organization is,
of its inherent nature, regarded by the rest of the world as a challenge; and they have been entitled by their experience to conclude
that their strength and cohesion both measure with pretty rigorous accuracy the respect they are likely to achieve. They have
suffered, as every new system suffers, from grave excess of bureauc-
ratism, and from the disease of orthodoxy. Their ruthlessness is,
in part, an inheritance of an evil tradition, in part the almost
inevitable technique of professional revolutionists who, unable
by their principles to compromise, are accustomed to regard their
lives as the stakes in the game. I know no evidence to suggest that
Trotsky would have been less stern than Stalin in dealing with
a challenge to his power; and the effective difference between
Stalin's victims and those of the Czar is that the whole world
regarded the latter as martyrs to a great cause. No such public
opinion has been aroused by the trials of the Soviet prisoners as
was aroused, for instance, by the execution of Sacco and Vanzetti,
or the trial of Dimitrov or the trial of Professor Furan in
Yugoslavia.

To see the problem, once more, in its proper perspective one
must think oneself back into a period like that of the Reformation.
Then, as now, two great systems of social organization were struggling for mastery. Protestantism did not establish itself in twenty
years. It took over a century and a quarter of bloody war for men
to accept the compromise of live and let live. The Soviet experiment goes deeper than that of the Reformation in the changes of
human behaviour it seeks to induce; it is not, I think, startling,
therefore, that Stalin and his colleagues should not yet be prepared
to relax their authority to permit its foundations to be called into
question. They confront, of course, the danger that they, like all
dictators, may be poisoned by the very volume of the power they

possess so that they cling to it as absolute even when the need for its rigour has gone. I do not deny that danger. I do not deny, either, that the rulers of the Soviet Union have attracted their full share of fools and sycophants about them. On the other side, there are some facts of significance to be borne in mind. The new Soviet Constitution may, with real peace, become an immense step forward; one, certainly, that in neither form nor content would Fascist dictators dare to emulate. The second fact is the immense number of ordinary men and women, not themselves members of the dominant Communist party, who share in the effective public administration of Soviet life. The third fact is the enjoyment by the ordinary worker of a luxury of criticism about the details of his working life which is of immense significance to him, and largely inaccessible to his fellows under the capitalist system. Anyone who has been present at a meeting of a factory soviet, or read the wall newspaper in a shop or factory, knows well enough that the Soviet worker is a free man in the work of his daily life in a sense to which few English or American trade unionists can pretend. And he has at his disposal a freedom of access to his cultural heritage unrivalled under any capitalist system. In general, moreover, he has two great assets denied to his fellows elsewhere. The fear of unemployment has been removed from his life; and he has a confidence that, given international peace, he and above all his children face a future that will consistently expand. He is still, no doubt, called upon for great sacrifices. But no one can visit the Soviet Union without the sense that its peoples feel themselves to be the masters of their own destiny in a way quite different from that realized by any other people.

On any showing, these are, I think, immense gains. They do not exclude the fact that the dictatorship still throws heavy shadows across the possible freedoms open to men. They do give reason to suppose that, as men and women in the Soviet Union become accustomed to the ways of a new civilization, the sense of their secure establishment will necessarily mean the relaxation of the dictatorship. The vital things are, first, the removal of the fear of

foreign intervention, with its corollary that Russian discontent
is thereby encouraged to conspiratorial relationships; and, second,
time enough for the mood to pass in which every opponent of the
men in power seems necessarily to be a revolutionary conspirator.
If critics like Trotsky announce that the first condition of Russian
salvation is the "removal" of the present leaders, that is an incite-
ment to reprisals which are bound to slow down the attainment
of an atmosphere in which a full right of free criticism emerges. If
America becomes hysterical about Soviet "expansionism," it slows
down the pace of Soviet democratization. Granted all the shadows,
the logic of the Russian system involves, in all normal circumstances, an ability to move forward to the revivification of principles of freedom.

That was not the case with the fascist dictatorships. By their
nature they involved the domination of the many in the interest
of the few; by their nature, also, they involved military adventure,
which means the perpetual strains and stresses of nations organized for war. The purpose of fascism is to prevent the relations of
production from coming into a natural harmony with the forces
of production; for that prevention, and increasingly, the method of
coercion is inescapable. Fascism has done nothing to deprive the
holders of economic power of their privileges, save where these
have been opponents of its policy. How should it do so, when its
exponents have been the allies of, and have been financed by,
the owners of economic power? It cannot permit the free expression of grievance; for, increasingly, this would be to admit the
hollowness of its claims. It dare not permit freedom of association;
were it to do so, its enemies would organize at once for battle
against it. There is, in short, no way open to a fascist dictatorship,
as in logic there is to the rulers of the Soviet Union, to transform
the processes of coercion into processes of consent. That ability
was at the disposal of capitalism in its epoch of expansion. With
the close of that epoch, it has either to fight democracy or to submit
to transformation by it. Fascism in all its forms chose the first
alternative; and over a wide area it registered victories. But there

was nothing of finality in their nature. There have been dark ages before in history; they mark the end of an economic system and the birth of a new. The fascist gloried in his uneasy hour of triumph. It was yet possible to discern in his vain glory the conscious fear of an impending doom.

3

One last word is necessary. I do not mean by the prediction that fascism contains the seeds of its own decay any assurance that its final downfall will come quickly or that the victory of 1945 will be a final one. No one who looks at our world need doubt the power of reaction to fight vigorously for its privileges, its power, also, as it declines, to destroy no inconsiderable part of civilization. We shall have to pay heavily for the power of reaction; do not let us forget that it took Germany until the nineteenth century to recover from the Thirty Years' War. The recovery of all Europe and Asia from the Second World War will be a long and hard task. We may have to pay so heavily that, as in the Soviet Union, men may have to pass through an iron age before the reign of freedom is re-established.

Our business is to be prepared for the eventualities, so to organize ourselves that those to whom freedom matters are powerful enough to abridge as much as possible the period of difficulty. Amid all their perplexities, they have ground for hope. For they are entitled to the knowledge that the impulses of men to affirm their own essence rise superior to every effort at suppression; even the slave will dream that one day he may be free. They have the right to emphasize that, if liberty is stricken, the conquests of science over nature are inhibited at every turn. They can be confident, also, that men, however ignorant, will not finally endure the paradox of poverty and unemployment in a society that might be rich and secure. They will need, indeed, great qualities if they are to win, courage above all, and the power to endure with resignation the bitterness of temporary defeat. They will require the self-control that gives rein to the heart only as it is guided by the mind. They will need philosophy as well as faith, daring not less than patience. It is the glory of freedom that it brings these qualities to those who serve it with fidelity. Before now, it has transformed a prison into an altar. Before now, it has brought the light of unconquerable hope into places that seemed utterly dark. We who fight the battle of freedom can maintain at least one certainty. We know that alone among the ends men seek it has the genius, where the need of its service is imperative, to give the quality of heroes to the common men who answer its call.

1937–47.   HAROLD J. LASKI

I. INTRODUCTORY

1

I MEAN by liberty the absence of restraint upon the existence of those social conditions which, in modern civilization, are the necessary guarantees of individual happiness. I seek to inquire into the terms upon which it is attainable in the Western world, and, more especially, to find those rules of conduct to which political authority must conform if men are, in a genuine sense, to be free.

Already, therefore, I am maintaining a thesis. I am arguing, first, that liberty is essentially an absence of restraint. It implies power to expand, the choice by the individual of his own way of life without imposed prohibitions from without. Men cannot, as Rousseau claimed, be forced into freedom. They do not, as Hegel insisted, find their liberty in obedience to the law. They are free when the rules under which they live leave them without a sense of frustration in realms they deem significant. They are unfree whenever the rules to which they have to conform compel them to conduct which they dislike and resent. I do not deny that there are types of conduct against which prohibitions are desirable: I ought, for instance, to be compelled, even against my wish, to educate my children. But I am arguing that any rule which demands from me something I would not otherwise give is a diminution of my freedom.

A second implication is important. My thesis involves the view that if in any state there is a body of men who possess unlimited political power, those over whom they rule can never be free. For

the one assured result of historical investigation is the lesson that
uncontrolled power is invariably poisonous to those who possess it.
They are always tempted to impose their canon upon others,
and, in the end, they assume that the good of the community
depends upon the continuance of their power. Liberty always
demands a limitation of political authority, and it is never attained unless the rulers of a state can, where necessary, be called
to account. That is why Pericles insisted that the secret of liberty
is courage.

By making liberty the absence of restraint, I make it, of course,
a purely negative condition. I do not thereby mean to assume that
a man will be happier the more completely restraints are absent
from the society to which he belongs. In a community like our own,
the pressure of numbers and the diversity of desires make necessary
both rules and compulsions. Each of these is a limitation upon
freedom. Some of them are essential to happiness, but that does
not for a moment make them less emphatically limitations. Our
business is to secure such a balance between the liberty we need
and the authority that is essential as to leave the average man with
the clear sense that he has elbow room for the continuous expression of his personality.

Nor must we confound liberty with certain other concepts without which it has no meaning. There may be absence of restraint
in the economic sphere, for example, in the sense that a man may
be free to enter any vocation he may choose. Yet if he is deprived
of security in employment he becomes the prey of a mental and
physical servitude incompatible with the very essence of liberty.
Nevertheless, economic security is not liberty, though it is a condition without which liberty is never effective. I do not mean that
those who can take their ease in Zion are thereby free men. Once
and for all, let us agree that property alone does not make a
man free. But those who know the normal life of the poor, their
perpetual fear of the morrow, their haunting sense of impending
disaster, their fitful search for a beauty which perpetually eludes
them, will realize well enough that, without economic security,

liberty is not worth having. Men may well be free and yet remain unable to realize the fruits of freedom.

Again, we live in a big world, about which, at our peril, we have to find our way. There can, under these conditions, be no freedom that is worth while unless the mind is trained to use its freedom. We cannot, otherwise, make explicit our experience of life, and so report to the centre of political decision the wants we derive from that experience. The right of the modern man to education became fundamental to his freedom once the mastery of nature by science transformed the sources of power. Deprive a man of knowledge, and the road to ever greater knowledge, and you will make him, inevitably, the slave of those more fortunate than himself. But deprivation of knowledge is not a denial of liberty. It is a denial of the power to use liberty for great ends. An ignorant man may be free even in his ignorance. In our world he cannot employ his freedom so as to give him assurance of happiness. A compulsory training of the mind is still compulsion. It is a temporary sacrifice of some liberty for the promise of a greater freedom in the future.

Two other preliminary remarks are important to the thesis I am urging. Everyone knows the danger to freedom which exists in any community where there is either special privilege on the one hand or what is termed the tyranny of the majority on the other. John Stuart Mill long ago pointed out that liberty was at first normally and naturally conceived as protection against the tyranny of the political rulers. The latter disposed of a power to which their subjects were compelled to conform; and it became vital in the interest of freedom to limit that power either by the recognition of special immunities or by the creation of constitutional guarantees. Even in the modern state the underlying substance of the argument may not be neglected. Power as such, when uncontrolled, is always the natural enemy of freedom. It prevents the exercise of those capacities which are released for activity by the absence of restraint. Wherever it is possessed in excess, it tilts the balance of social action in favour of its possessors.

A franchise limited to the owners of property means legislation in
the interests of that class. The exclusion of a race or creed from a
share in citizenship is, invariably, its exclusion also from the benefits of social action. In any state, therefore, where liberty is to move
to its appointed end, it is important that there should be equality.

Now equality is not the same thing as liberty. I do not, indeed,
agree with Lord Acton's famous dictum that the "passion for
equality makes vain the hope of freedom"; [1] liberty and equality
are not so much antithetic as complementary. Men might be
broadly equal under a despotism, and yet be unfree. But it is, I
think, historically true that in the absence of certain equalities
complete freedom can never hope for realization. The acute mind
of Aristotle long ago saw that the craving for equality is one of the
most profound roots of revolution. The reason is clear enough.
The absence of equality means special privilege for some and not
for others, special privilege which is not, so to say, in nature but
in a deliberate contrivance of the social environment. Men like
Harrington and Madison and Marx all insisted, and with truth,
that whatever the forms of state, political power would, in fact,
belong to the owners of economic power. We need not argue that
our happiness depends upon the possession of political power;
we can argue that exclusion from political power is likely to mean
exclusion from that which largely determines the contours of happiness. And it follows that the more equal are the social rights
of citizens, the more likely those citizens are to be able to utilize
their freedom in realms worthy of exploration. Certainly the
history of the abolition of special privilege has been, also, the
history of the expansion of opportunities for the common man.
The more equality there is in a free state, the more use, in general,
we can make of our freedom.

Here, perhaps, it is worth while for a moment to dwell upon
the meaning of equality. Nothing is easier than to make it a

[1] Acton, *The History of Freedom and Other Essays* (London: Macmillan and
Company, 1922), p. 57.

notion utterly devoid of all common sense.[2] It does not mean identity of treatment. The ultimate fact of the variety of human nature, our differences of both hereditary capacity and social nurture, this is inescapable. To treat men as different as Newton and Byron, Cromwell and Rousseau, in a precisely similar way is patently absurd. But equality does not mean identity of treatment. It implies an insistence that there is no difference inherent in nature between the claims of men to happiness. It therefore requires that society shall not construct against those claims barriers which weigh more heavily upon some than upon others. It shall not exclude men from the legal profession because they are black or Wesleyans or Freemasons. It shall not deny access to the courts to men whose opinions society in general disapproves. The idea of equality is obviously an idea of levelling. It implies an attempt to give each man a chance as similar as possible to those of other men to utilize what powers he may possess. It means that he is to have a voice in the framing of decisions which affect him, that whatever legal rights inhere in any other man as a citizen shall inhere in him also; that where different treatments are meted out by society to different persons, the differences shall be capable of explanation in terms of the common good. It means the recognition of the urgent need of all—for food, for instance, and clothing, and shelter—before there is special recognition of non-urgent claims in any.

Equality, so regarded, seems to me inescapably connected with freedom. For, in the first place, it seems to mean the organization of opportunities; and, in the second place, it means that no man's opportunities are sacrificed, except on terms of social principle, to the claims of another. Let me illustrate by a simple example. On the view I am taking, no child could be deprived of education that another might receive it; but in a choice of men, say, for a post in the Treasury, one might be preferred to another on the

[2] As Mr. Aldous Huxley, for instance, does with a quite unnecessary apparatus of scholarship in his *Proper Studies* (Garden City: Doubleday, Doran and Company, 1928), pp. 1–31.

ground of ability or character or training. The idea of equality, in a word, implies such an organization of opportunity that no man's personality suffers frustration to the private benefit of others. He is given a chance to use his freedom to experiment with his powers. He knows that no barriers impede him in his effort to attain happiness more than they impede others. He may not win his objective, but at least he cannot claim that society has so weighted the scale against him as to assure his defeat.

The second consideration I have noted will take us further afield. It is often argued that a theory of liberty which starts from the effort of the individual to attain happiness must break down because it fails to remember that society also has rights, and that these are necessarily superior to those of its component parts. Any organization, it is said, is more than the units of which it is composed. A nation-state like America or England is not merely a body of Englishmen or Americans, but something beyond them. It has a life and a reality, needs and purposes, which are not exhausted by the sum of the needs and purposes of its individual members. The liberty of each citizen is born of, and must be subordinated to, the liberty of that greater whole from which much of his meaning is derived. For the rights of each of us depend upon the protective rampart of social organization. It is because the state enforces our rights as obligations upon others that we have the opportunity to enjoy them. We are free, it is said, not for ourselves but for the society which gives us meaning. Where our interests conflict with the obviously greater interest of the society, we ourselves must give way.

It is, I think, true to say that an individual abstracted from society and regarded as entitled to freedom outside its environment is devoid of meaning. None of us is Crusoe or St. Simeon Stylites on his pillar. We are born to live our lives in London or New York, Paris or Berlin or Rome. Our liberty has to be realized in a welter of competing and co-operating interests which achieve rational co-ordination only by something not unlike a miracle. The necessity to give way to others, to accept, that is, restraint upon our right to unfettered activity, is inherent in the nature of things. But the surrender we make is a surrender not for the sake of the society regarded as something other than its members, but exactly and precisely for men and women whose totality is conveniently summarized in a collective and abstract noun. I do not understand how England, for instance, can have an end or purpose different from, or opposed to, the end or purpose of its citizens. We strive to do our duty to England for the sake of Englishmen living and to come; a duty to England separate from them, and in which they do not share, is surely inconceivable.

Or, at least, it would be inconceivable, were it not that perhaps the most influential theory of the state in our own time has been built upon it. What is termed the idealist theory of the state is, broadly, the argument that individual freedom means obedience to the law of the society to which I belong. My personality, it is said, is simply an expression of the organized whole. When I say that I am seeking to realize myself, I mean in fact that I am seeking to be one with the order of which I am a part. I am not independent of, or isolated in, that order, but one with it. As it realizes itself, so am I also realized. The greater and more powerful it becomes, the greater and more powerful do I become as a consequence. The more fully, therefore, I serve it, the more fully do I express myself. Liberty so conceived is so far from being an absence of restraint that it is essentially subordination to a system of rational purposes which receive their highest expression in the activity of the state. To be one with that activity may well then be regarded as the highest freedom a citizen can know.

In the whole history of political philosophy there is nothing more subtle than the skill with which the idealist school has turned the flank of the classic antithesis between liberty and authority. From the Greeks to Rousseau it was always conceived that a man's freedom is born of a limitation upon what his rulers may exact from him; since Rousseau, and, more particularly, since Hegel, it has been urged that conformity to a code, and even compulsory obedience to it, is the very essence of freedom. So startling a paradox needs, at the least, explanation. Liberty, it argues, is not a mere negative thing like absence of restraint. It is rather a positive self-determination of the will which in each of us seeks the fulfilment of a rational purpose that lies behind, and gives unified meaning to, the diversified chaos of purposes in each of us. We desire freedom, that is to say, in order that we may be ourselves at our best. The right object of our wills, the thing which, did we know all the facts, we would truly desire, is clearly that for which we would seek freedom. Our real will, and the highest part of ourselves, seeks this object. This will, moreover, is the same in each member of society; for, at bottom, the real will is a common will which finds its highest embodiment in the state. In this view, therefore, the state is the highest part of ourselves. For it represents in its will what each of us would seek to be if the temporary, the immediate, and the irrational were stripped from the objects we desire. Its object is what alone we should aim at were we free to will only our permanent good. It is, so to say, the long and permanent end that, in the ultimate analysis, we come individually to will after private experience of wrong direction and erroneous desire. The more intimately, therefore, we make our will one with that of the state, the more completely are we free. The nature of the social bond makes service to its demands the very essence of freedom.

Before I seek to analyse this view, I would point out how simply this argument enables us to resolve the very difficult problem of social obligation. When I obey the state, I obey the best part of myself. The more fully I discover its purposes, the more fully, also, is revealed to me their identity with that at which, in the long view, I aim. So that when I obey it, I am, in fact, obeying myself; in a real sense its commands are my own. Its view is built upon the innumerable intelligences from the interplay of which social organization derives its ultimate form; obviously such a view is superior in its wisdom to the result my own petty knowledge can attain. My true liberty is, therefore, a kind of permanent tutelage to the state, a sacrifice of my limited purpose to its larger end upon the ground that, as this larger end is realized, I, too, am given realization. I may, in fact, be most fully free when I am most suffused with the sense of compulsion.

To me, at least, this view contradicts all the major facts of experience. It seems to me to imply not only a paralysis of the will, but a denial of that uniqueness of individuality, that sense that each of us is different from his fellows, that is the ultimate fact of human experience. For as I encounter the state, it is for me a body of men issuing orders. Most of them I can obey either with active goodwill or, at least, with indifference. But I may encounter some one order, a demand, for instance, for military service, or a compulsion to abandon my religious faith, which seems to me in direct contradiction to the whole scheme of values I have found in life. How I can be the more free by subordinating my judgment of right to one which is directly opposed to that judgment, I cannot understand. If the individual is not to find the source of his decisions in the contact between the outer world and himself, in the experience, that is, which is the one thing that separates him from the rest of society, he ceases to have meaning as an individual in any sense that is creative. For the individual is real to himself not by reason of the contacts he shares with others, but because he reaches those contacts through a channel which he alone can know. His true self is the self that is isolated from his fellows and that contributes the fruit of isolated meditation to the common good which, collectively, they seek to bring into being.

A true theory of liberty, I urge, is built upon a denial of each of the assumptions of idealism. My true self is not a selected system of rational purposes identical with those sought by every member of society. We cannot split up the wholeness of personality in this way. My true self is all that I am and do. It is the total impression produced by the bewildering variety of my acts, good and bad and indifferent. All of them go to the formation of my view of the universe; all of them are my expression of my striving to fulfil my personality. Each, while it is, is real, and each, as real, must give way only in terms of a judgment I make, not of one made for me by some other will, if I am to remain a purposive human being serving myself as an end. This attempt, in a word, at the extraction of a partial self from the whole of my being as alone truly myself not only denies that my experience is real, but also makes me merely an instrument to the purpose of others. Whatever that condition is, surely it cannot be recognized as freedom.

But we can go further than this. I see no reason to suppose that this assumed real will is identical in every member of society. The ultimate and inescapable fact in politics is the variety of human wills. There is no continuum which makes all of them one. Experience suggests common objects of desire, but each will that wills these common objects is a different will in every sense not purely metaphorical. We all have a will to international peace. But the unity these wills make is not one will but a fusion of separate wills to the attainment of a common purpose. And we must remember that in every society the objects of wills cannot, in some mystic fashion, be fused into a higher unity somehow compounded of them all. I see no meaning, for instance, in the statement that the antithetic purposes of Jesuits and Freemasons are somehow transcended in a higher purpose which includes them both; that is to say that a Jesuit or a Freemason is most truly himself when he ceases to be himself, which, frankly, seems to me nonsense. A member of the Praesidium of the Third International whose will aims supremely at the overthrow of capitalism is not somehow at one with the will of the President of the British Federation of Industries, to whom all the purposes of the Third International are anathema. Both, doubtless, will the good; but the point is that each wills the good as he sees it, and each would regard the fulfilment of the other's ideal of good as a definite destruction of his own. There is, therefore, no single and common will in society, unless we mean thereby the vague concept, entirely useless for political philosophy, that men desire the good. Each of us desires the good as he sees it; and each of us sees a good derived from an individual and separate experience into which no other person can fully enter. Our connection with others is, at the best, partial and interstitial. Our pooling of experiences to make a common purpose somewhere is in no case other than fragmentary. We remain ourselves even when we join with others to attain some common object of desire. The ultimate isolation of the individual personality is the basis from which any adequate theory of politics must start.

I reject, therefore, the idea of a real will, and, still more, the idea that there is an *a priori* common will in society. It is a logical inference that I should reject also the doctrine that all state action is at bottom the exercise of the real will of society. For, first of all, I see no reason to suppose that social life is ultimately the product of a single and rational mind organizing its activities in terms of a logical process. To speak of the "mind of society" seems to me merely a metaphorical way of describing a course of action which is made valid by translation into fact. There are no governing principles in social life deliberately emerging from the interplay of its myriad constituent parts. Governing principles emerge; but they emerge through the wills of individual minds. And the state is magnified to excess when it is regarded as embodying a unified will. The state is a complex of rulers and subjects territorially organized and seeking, by the conferment of power upon those rulers, effective co-ordination of social activities. The rulers exercise the right to use force, if necessary, to that end. But no one, I think, can examine the course of history and say that the experience of any state indicates a permanent embodiment of the highest good we know in the purpose of the state. Our rulers, doubtless, aim at the good as they see it. Yet what they see as good may not be so recognizable to us, and may well provoke in us the sense that life would not be worth living if their view were to prevail. The unity of the state, in a word, is not inherently there. It is made by civic acceptance of what its rulers propose. It is not necessarily good because it is accepted; it is not necessarily right because it is proposed. Obedience ought always to depend on the substance contained in the rules made by government; it is a permanent essay in the conditional mood.[3]

Here, of course, the idealist retorts that he is dealing not with the states of history, but with the state as such; he is concerned with the "pure" instance and not with deviations from the ideal.[4] But it is with actual states that we have to deal in everyday life as we know it, with states whose policy is directed by men who are human like ourselves. The policy they announce must, obviously, be subject to our scrutiny; and our judgment is necessarily made out of an experience not identical with, even though it be similar to, theirs. I cannot believe that a theory fits the facts of history which assumes that a policy is going to be right, whatever it is; and that freedom will be found only in acceptance of it. I do not believe that the Huguenot of 1685 was made the more free by accepting, against his conscience, the Revocation; nor do I believe that Luther would have been more free had he accepted the decrees of Rome and abandoned his protest. Man is one among many, obstinately refusing reduction to unity. His separateness, his isolation, are indefeasible; indeed, they are so fundamental that they are the basis on which his civic obligations are built. He cannot abandon the consequences of his isolation, which are, broadly speaking, that his experience is private, and the will built out of that experience personal to himself. If he surrenders his will to others, he surrenders his personality. If his will is set by the will of others, he ceases to be master of himself. I cannot believe that a man no longer master of himself is in any real sense free.

2

If we reject a view which, like that just considered, seeks to dissolve the reality of the individual into the society of which he

[3] All this has been put in classic form by the late Professor Hobhouse in his *Metaphysical Theory of the State* (New York: The Macmillan Company, 1918).
[4] Cf. Ernest Barker, *Political Thought in England from Herbert Spencer to the Present Day* (New York: Henry Holt and Company, 1915), p. 80.

is a part, what are we left with as a pattern within which a man
seeks freedom? Let us try and draw a picture of the place of
man in a community like our own. He finds himself involved in
a complex of relationships out of which he must form such a
pattern of conduct as will give him happiness. There are his
family, his friends, the church to which he may belong, his voluntary association—trade union, employers' association, or whatever it may be—and there is the state. All of these, save the state,
he may in greater or less degree avoid. A man may cut himself
off from family or friends; he may refuse membership of a church
or vocational body; he cannot refuse membership of the state.
Somewhere or other he encounters it as a body of persons issuing
orders, and he is involved in the problem of deciding whether or
not he will obey those orders. The point I want to make at the
moment is this: every order issued is, in a final analysis, issued
by a person or persons to another person or persons. When we
say, in such a complex of relationships as this, that a man is free,
what do we mean? We know that if his church issues an order to
him of which he disapproves, he can leave his church; so, too, with
all other bodies save the state. The latter can, if he seeks evasion
of its commands, use compulsion to secure obedience to its orders.
It makes, we say, the law, and a member of the state is legally
compelled to obey the law.

But he is not free, as I have argued, merely because he obeys the
law. His freedom, in relation to the law, depends on the effect of
any particular order upon his experience. He is seeking happiness;
some order seems to him a wanton invasion of that happiness. He
may be right or wrong in so thinking; the point of fact is that
he has no alternative but to go by his own moral certainties. Now
freedom exists in a state where a man knows that the decisions
made by the ultimate authority do not invade his personality. The
conditions of freedom are then those which assure the absence of
such invasions. The citizen who asks for freedom is entitled to the
conditions which, collectively, are the guarantees that he will be
able to go on the road to his happiness, as he conceives it, un-

hindered. Neither conditions nor guarantees will ever be perfect; nor will they ever cover all upon which happiness depends. The state, for instance, may say that I may marry the woman I love; it cannot say that she will marry me if I so desire. The freedom it secures to me is the absence of a barrier in the way of marriage if I can win her consent.

From this angle, liberty may appropriately be resolved into a system of liberties. There are realms of conduct within which, to be free, I must be permitted to act as I please; to be denied self-expression there is to be denied freedom. What we need to know is, I suggest, first what those realms of conduct are, and, second, what my duty as a citizen is when I am, in any one of them, prohibited from acting as I please. The difficulty here, of course, is impossible to exaggerate. It is the problem of knowing when a man ought deliberately to make up his mind to break the law or to refuse obedience to it. In the idealist theory, this problem does not arise; it is answered *a priori* by the definition of freedom as obedience to the law. But because we have rejected this view, we have to admit that there will be occasional disobedience, at the least, and that this may be justified. We have to discover the principles of its justification.

Liberty, I have said, may be resolved into a system of liberties; and from this angle it may be said that it is the purpose of social organization to see to it that this system is adequately safeguarded. How can the state, which charges itself with the function of supreme co-ordination, properly fulfil this task? How can it guarantee to me such an environment for my activity that I do not suffer frustration in my search for happiness?

There have been many answers to this question, some of them of the highest interest and importance. One or two I wish to consider, partly because of their significance in themselves, and partly because, from that consideration, I wish to make the inference that no merely mechanical arrangements will ever secure permanent freedom to the citizens of a state. While there are certain constitutional forms which are, I think, essential to freedom, their mere presence as forms will not of itself suffice to make men free. I shall seek, further, to draw the conclusion that, whatever the form of social organization, liberty is essentially an expression of an impalpable atmosphere among men. It is a sense that in the things we deem significant there is the opportunity of continuous initiative, knowledge that we can, so to speak, experiment with ourselves, think differently or act differently from our neighbours without danger to our happiness. We are not free, that is, unless we can form a plan of conduct to suit our own character without social penalties. Freedom is in an important degree a matter of law; but in a degree not less important it is a matter, also, of the *mores* of society when these *mores* lie outside the sphere within which law can operate.

You will observe that I am still, from the angle of political organization, thinking of liberty as a safeguard of the individual against those who rule him. I do so for the best of reasons. Whoever exerts power in a community is tempted to the abuse of power. Even in a democracy, we must have ways and means of protecting the minority against a majority which seeks to invade its freedom. Mankind has suffered much from the assumption that, once the people has become master in its own house, there is no limit to its power. You have only to remember the history of racial minorities like the Negroes, of religious or national minorities like Jews and Czechs, to realize that democracy, of itself, is no guarantee of freedom. This raises the larger question of whether freedom in the modern state can ever be satisfactorily secured by internal sanctions, and whether, in fact, it is ever durably possible save in the terms of a strong and stable international organization. For, clearly, we must not think of freedom as involving only an individual as opposed to the community; it involves also the freedom of groups, racial, ecclesiastical, vocational, as opposed to the community and the state; it involves also the relation of states to one another, as, for instance, in the problem of annexation. No English-

man would think himself free if his domestic life were defined
for him by another state; and no honourable Frenchman but had
a bitter sense of unfreedom during the Nazi occupation of French
soil. Our generation, at least, is unlikely to underestimate the
problem of what limits may be set to the demand for freedom by
a national group.

3

Everyone who considers the relation of liberty to the institutions
of a state will, I think, find it difficult to resist the conclusion that
without democracy there cannot be liberty. That is not an over-
popular thesis in our time. A reaction against democratic ideals
is the fashion, and critics of these ideals, whose attacks are often
disguised as defence, are earnest in maintaining democracy's obsolescence. Yet consider, for a moment, what democracy implies.
It involves a frame of government in which, first, men are given
the chance of making the government under which they live; in
which, also, the laws that government promulgates are binding
equally upon all. I do not think the average man can be made
happy merely by living in a democracy: I do not see how he can
avoid a sense of continuous frustration unless he does. For if he
does not share in making the government, if he cannot, where his
fellows so choose, be himself made one of the rulers of the state,
he is excluded from that which assures him that his experience
counts. To read the history of England before the enfranchisement
of the wage earner is to realize that however small is the value of
the franchise it still assures the attention of government to grievance. The right to the franchise is therefore essential to liberty;
and a citizen excluded from it is unfree. Unfree for the simple
reason that the rulers of the state will not regard his will as entitled
to consideration in the making of policy. They will do things for
him, but not those things he himself regards as urgent—as Parliament a hundred years ago met the grim problem of urban want
by building more churches to the glory of the Lord. Whatever is to

be said against the democratic form of the state, it seems to me unquestionable that it has forced the needs of humble men on the attention of government in a way impossible under any other form.

To be free, I argue, a people must be able to choose its rulers at stated intervals simply because there is no other way in which their wants, as they experience those wants, will receive attention. It is fundamental to the conference of power that it should never be permanent. If it is so, it ceases to give attention to the purposes for which it is conferred and thinks only of the well-being of those who can exercise it. That has been, notably, the history of monarchy and aristocracy, and, in general, of the practice of colonial dominion. Power that is unaccountable makes instruments of men who should be ends in themselves. A responsible government lives always in the shadow of coming defeat; and this makes it eager to satisfy those with whose destinies it is charged.

This is a general principle which, stated so baldly, does not adequately illustrate the substance it implies. The history of the struggle for popular freedom has given us knowledge of certain rules in the organization of a state the presence of which is fundamental to freedom. It can, I think, be shown that no citizen is secure in liberty unless certain rights are guaranteed to him, rights which the government of the state cannot hope permanently to overthrow; and unless, to secure the maintenance of those rights, there is a separation of the judicial from the executive power.

Let me take the second of these principles first. The citizens of a state choose men to make the laws under which they are to live. It is urgent that these should be binding upon all without fear or favour; that I, for instance, should be able to live secure in the knowledge that their application to me will not differ from their application to others. Clearly enough, in the modern state, the application of law to life demands a vast body of civil servants to administer it. Not the least important problem of our time is that which arises when the legality of their administration is in question. In Anglo-Saxon communities it has been regarded as elementary that the interpretation of law should be entrusted to an independent body of officials—the judges—who can arbitrate impartially between government and citizens. That view I take to be of the first importance to freedom; and its acceptance involves considerations which we must examine in some detail.

The business of a judiciary, broadly speaking, is the impartial interpretation of the law as between government and citizen, or between individuals or classes of citizens who dispute with one another. The government, for instance, charges a man with treason; obviously he is deprived of something essential to his freedom if the law is strained so as to make of treason something it in fact is not, in order to cover the acts which the government seeks to have accepted as treason. Here, obviously, the judge must be assured that his own independence may be maintained with safety to himself. He must not suffer in his person or position because of the view he takes. It must not be within the power of either the government or other persons to deprive him of his authority because, as best he may, he applies the law. This, I think, makes it essential that all judicial appointments should be held during good behaviour. There may be an age-limit of service, of course; but, this apart, nothing should permit the removal of a judge from the bench except corruption or physical or mental unfitness. I do not, therefore, believe that a judicial system founded upon popular election is a satisfactory way of choosing judges, the more so if submission to re-election is involved; and the system, abandoned in England in 1701, of making judicial appointment dependent upon the pleasure of government is equally indefensible. Once a man has been appointed to judicial office nothing must stand in the way of his complete independence of mind. Election, re-election, a power in the government to dismiss, are all of them incompatible with the function the judge is to perform. They will not, as a general rule, either give us the men we want, or enable us to keep them when we have found them.

But we must, I think, go further than this. Judicial independence is not merely a matter of mechanical technique; it is also psychological in character. The judge whose promotion is dependent upon the will of the executive, even more, the judge who may look to a political career as a source of future distinction, neither of these is adequately protected in that independence of mind which is the pivot of his function. No less a person than Mr. Chief Justice Taft has told us that as President he appointed a predecessor Chief Justice at least partly because he approved of one of his decisions.[5] No one could, I think, have confidence in the bench if it were known that decisions pleasing to a given political party might lead either to promotion or to being chosen a presidential candidate or Lord Chancellor. It seems to me, therefore, that we must so organize the method of judicial promotion as to prevent the executive from choosing only men of its own outlook, and, further, see to it that appointment to the bench is definitely taken as the end of a political career. These are problems of detailed technique into which I cannot now enter; [6] here I am concerned only to point out that the problem of independence which they raise is one that it is necessary to meet with frankness.

But the judge's authority as a safeguard of our freedom is in the modern state threatened in another way. Modern legislation is so huge both in volume and extent that the average assembly has neither time nor energy to scrutinize its details. The modern habit is, therefore, to pass acts which confer a general power, and to leave the filling in of details to the discretion of the department concerned. To this, I think, no one can really take exception. The state must do its work; and it must develop the agencies necessary to that end. But I think we have grave reason for fear when the growth of this delegated legislative authority is accompanied with, or followed by, the conferring of powers upon government departments themselves to determine the question of whether the powers they take are legal or not. I regard the growth of delegated legisla-

[5] W. H. Taft, *Our Chief Magistrate and His Powers* (New York: Columbia University Press, 1916), pp. 102–103.

[6] See my detailed discussion of the point in *Studies in Law and Politics* (New Haven: Yale University Press, 1932).

tion as both necessary and desirable; but if it is not gravely to impair our freedom, it should, I think, be developed only under the amplest safeguards.

Decisions, for instance, like that on the Ju Toy case [7] in the United States, and on *Arlidge* v. *Local Government Board* [8] in England, may clearly become a real menace to the liberty of the citizen, unless there are genuine safeguards against their abuse. They suggest a type of executive justice for which the methods of the Star Chamber are the nearest analogy. No body of civil servants, however liberal-minded they may be, ought to be free both to make the law and to devise the procedure by which its legality may be tested—and that, be it remembered, without a power of appeal from their decision. It may be taken for granted that the modern state needs an administrative law; in matters, for instance, like rate fixing in public utilities, in workmen's compensation cases, in matters concerning public health, the views of a body of experts in a public department are generally at least as valid as that of the judicial body. But one wants to be certain that in arriving at his decision the expert has been compelled to take account of all the relevant evidence; that the parties to his decision have had their day in court. This seems to me to involve the organization of a procedure for all administrative tribunals which takes account of the lessons we have learned both from the procedure of ordinary courts and from the history of the law of evidence; and it involves an appeal from administrative tribunals to a supreme administrative tribunal on all questions where denial of proper procedure is held to involve a denial of proper consideration. Something of this, if I understand the matter aright, has been granted to the American citizen by the Supreme Court in *McCall Ec.* v. *New York;* [9] and I should feel happier about the future of administrative law if I were certain that the principles of that decision applied to all governmental activities of the kind.

[7] 189 U.S. 253.
[8] (1915) A.C. 120.
[9] 38 Sup. Ct. Rep. 122.

Another safeguard is not less essential. We agree, for the most part, that the opinion of a single judge, even when reinforced by the verdict of a jury, ought not to be final in either criminal or civil cases. I should like to see that agreement extended to the sphere of administrative law. Where, that is to say, a departmental tribunal has rendered its decision, I should like an appeal to be possible to a higher administrative tribunal composed not only of officials, but also of laymen of experience in the matters involved who could be trusted to bring independent minds to the settlement of the matter in dispute. English experience of tribunals like the Civil Service Division of the Industrial Court, and the Commissioners of Income Tax, convinces me that the common sense of a good lay mind is, in this realm, an immense safeguard against departmental error. And we must remember that, however great be the goodwill of the public services, what to them may seem a simple matter of administrative routine, may be to the citizens involved a denial of the very substance of freedom. Certainly a case like *ex parte O'Brien* [10] makes one see how real would be the threat to public liberty if departmental legislation grew without proper judicial scrutiny at every stage of its development.

The problem, however, does not merely end here. There are two other sides of administrative action in which the uncontrolled power of the state is an implicit threat to civic freedom. Of the first, I would say here only a word, since I have treated it fully elsewhere. [11] The modern state is a sovereign state and therefore there are realms of its conduct where wrong on its part cannot imply the invocation by the citizen of penalty. The right to sue the state in tort seems to me quite fundamental to freedom. The modern state is in essence a public service corporation. Like any other body, it acts through servants who take decisions in its name. I can see no reason in the world why, like any other body

[10] (1923) 2 K.B. 61. (The Crown Proceeding Act, 1947, to a considerable degree has now remedied this situation by permitting the citizen to sue the crown over a wide area of action.)

[11] Cf. my *Grammar of Politics* (London: George Allen & Unwin Ltd.), pp. 541 ff.

serving the public, it should not be responsible for the torts of its
agents. If I am run over by the negligent driver of a railway truck,
I can secure damages; I do not see why I am not equally entitled
to damages if the truck is the property of, and is driven for, the
Postmaster General of His Majesty.[12]

But, still in the context of administration, the needs of liberty
go yet further. There has accumulated today about the departments of state a type of discretionary power which seems to me
full of danger unless it is exercised under proper safeguards.
Examples are the power of the Postmaster General of the United
States over the mails and of the Home Secretary in England over
requests from aliens for naturalization. Let me deal with the latter
authority, since I am better acquainted with its character. An
alien applies to the Home Secretary for naturalization. He answers
innumerable questions, and presents certificates of good character
from citizens who testify on oath to his standing. He has resided
in the country for at least five years and he will not, of course,
normally venture to apply unless his record is adequate. A request
is published in the press for any information about him, and,
after a due interval, the Home Secretary makes a decision about
the case. He has, of course, pursued his own inquiries, and he has,
presumably, received information about the applicant, upon
which his action is based. Now the point that disturbs me is
the fact that where a certificate of naturalization is refused, the
grounds for rejection are never, even privately to the applicant,
made known. He is refused privileges which may be vital to him
and to his family on the ground of accusations which may, doubtless, be true, but may also be completely without foundation and
capable, were opportunity afforded, of being immediately and
decisively refuted. And so great is the discretionary power of the
Minister that he may even substitute his own will for that of the
legislature. The Naturalization Act, for instance, demands a five-
year period of residence. A former Home Secretary, Lord Brent-
ford, announced that while he was in office he would grant no

[12] *Ibid.*

certificate unless the applicant had resided in England continuously for a period of thirteen years. It seems to me that this power to deny admission to citizenship, as it is exercised, is a complete negation of natural justice. No person ought to be condemned by accusations he is not given the opportunity to refute. Anyone who wishes to give testimony in a case of this kind ought surely to prove his *bona fides* by submitting to cross-examination from the applicant or his representative. I should like, therefore, to see the possibility of an appeal from the decision of the Home Secretary to a judge in chambers, where the latter would, on a case stated by the department, hear such evidence as the applicant chose to bring for its refutation and then only make a final decision. Anything less than this seems to me a wanton abuse of freedom; and, *mutatis mutandis,* this type of safeguard seems to me urgent wherever a minister is given a discretionary power which affects the liberty of the subject.

I accept, therefore, the traditional notion that the separation of the judicial from the executive power, the right of the former to determine the legality of executive decision, is the normal basis of freedom. I do not, however, believe that the separation of the executive from the legislature is either necessary or desirable. The origin of the idea is in the historic misinterpretation of the British Constitution by Montesquieu [13] and this, in its turn, was due to his misapplication of certain classic dicta of Locke.[14] The fact is that a separation in this realm results in a complete and undesirable erosion of responsibility. The British system, in which the executive, as a committee of the legislature, formulates its plans, which are accepted or rejected, has, I think, the clear advantage of showing the electorate exactly where responsibility for action must lie. Where mistakes are made, where there is corruption or dishonesty or abuse, these can be brought home forthwith to their authors. In the American system, that is not the case. The president is neither the master nor the servant of

13 *Esprit des Lois,* Bk. XI, Chap. VI.
14 Second Treatise, Sec. 12.

the legislature. The latter can make its own schemes; where its views—indeed, where its party complexion—are different from his, there is a constant tendency to paralysis of administration. Each can blame the other for failure. No clear policy emerges upon which the electorate can form a straightforward judgment. Independence makes for antagonism, and antagonism, in its turn, makes for confusion. Such a separation means, almost invariably, the construction of a separate quasi-executive in the legislature, which has an interest of its own distinct from, and often hostile to, that of the president.[15] I can see no necessary safeguard of liberty in this. The British system, where the executive may be at any moment destroyed by the legislature as a penalty for error or wrong, where, also, there lies always the prospect of an immediate and direct appeal to the people as the ultimate and only arbiter of difference, seems to me far more satisfactory.

4

Another institutional mechanism for the safeguarding of freedom is that of a bill of rights. Certain principles, freedom of speech, protection from arbitrary arrest, and the like, are regarded as especially sacred. They may be enshrined in a document which cannot constitutionally be invaded by either the legislature or the executive, save by a special procedure to which access is difficult. The First Amendment to the American Constitution, for example, stipulates that Congress shall pass no law abridging freedom of speech; and any act of Congress which touches upon the matter can be challenged for unconstitutionality before the Supreme Court. The amendment, moreover, cannot be repealed save by the usual process of constitutional change in America; and that means that, except in the event of an American revolution, it is unlikely ever to be directly attacked at all.

My own years of residence in the United States have convinced

[15] Cf. my paper on American federalism in the volume entitled *The Dangers of Obedience and Other Essays* (New York: Harper and Brothers, 1930).

me that there is a real value in bills of rights which it is both easy
and mistaken to underestimate. Granted that the people are
educated to an appreciation of their purpose, they serve to draw
attention, as attention needs to be drawn, to the fact that vigilance
is essential in the realm of what Cromwell called fundamentals.
Bills of rights are, quite undoubtedly, a check upon possible
excess in the government of the day. They warn us that certain
popular powers have had to be fought for, and may have to be
fought for again. The solemnity they suggest serves to set the
people on their guard. It acts as a rallying-point in the state for
all who care deeply for the ideals of freedom. I believe, for instance,
that the existence of the First Amendment has drawn innumerable
American citizens to defend freedom of speech who have no atom
of sympathy with the purposes for which it is used. A bill of
rights, so to say, canonizes the safeguards of freedom, and thereby
persuades men to worship at the altar who might not otherwise
note its existence.

All this, I think, is true; but it does not for a moment imply
that a bill of rights is an automatic guarantee of liberty. For the
relationship of legislation to its substance has to be measured
by the judiciary. Judges, after all, are human beings, likely, as
the rest of us, to be swept off their feet by gusts of popular passion.
The First Amendment to the American Constitution guarantees
freedom of speech and peaceable assembly; the Fourth Amendment legally secures to the citizen that his house shall not be
searched except upon a warrant of probable cause; the Eighth
Amendment legally secures him against excessive bail. Yet in one
hysterical week in 1919 the action of the executive power rendered
all these amendments worthless; [16] and the Fifteenth Amendment,
which sought political freedom for the coloured citizens of the
South, has never been effectively applied either by the executive
or by the courts.

[16] Cf. Louis Post, *The Deportations Delirium of 1920* (Chicago: C. H. Kerr
and Company, 1923). It is lamentable that a similar wave of hysteria has swept
over the United States twenty-five years later.

The fact is that any bill of rights depends for its efficacy on the determination of the people that it shall be maintained. It is just as strong, and no more, as the popular will to freedom. No one now doubts that the Espionage Acts were strained so as to destroy almost all that the First Amendment was intended to cover; that most of the charges preferred under it were, on their face, ludicrous. Yet you will remember that in *Abrams* v. *United States* [17] two judges stood alone in their insistence that the First Amendment really meant something; the judgment of the others was caught in the meshes of war hysteria. No principle is better established than the right of the citizen, under proper circumstances, to a writ of habeas corpus; that is, perhaps, the ark of the covenant in the Anglo-American conception of freedom. But who can ever forget the noble and pathetic words of Chief Justice Taney, in *ex parte Merryman*,[18] where he insists that the applicant is entitled to the writ and that, in view of President Lincoln's suspension of it—a suspension entirely illegal in character—he could not secure to Mr. Merryman his due rights? And let us remember, also, that even where the judge is prepared to do his duty, he cannot, in a period of excitement, count upon public opinion. Nothing is clearer than the fact that those who hanged Mr. Gordon during the Jamaica riots were guilty of murder. The opinion of Chief Justice Cockburn could not have made the issue more clear; it is a landmark in the judicial history of freedom. Yet the jury at once, in its despite, acquitted the accused. There have been, further, many occasions when breaches of fundamental principles of freedom, breaches which, on any showing, have been quite indefensible, have been followed at once by acts of indemnity. I know of only one case in England in the last hundred years in which such an act has been refused. Yet it is, I think, obvious that unless such breaches are definitely and deliberately punished, they will always occur on critical occasions. At such times it is impossible to trust those who are charged with

[17] 250 U.S. T's 616.
[18] See Taney's *Report*.

the exercise of power; and only the knowledge that swift and certain punishment will follow its abuse will make our rulers attentive to the needs of freedom.

I speak the language of severity; and I am anxious to stress that the language of severity is not that of the extremist. I invite you, as the proof of what I say, to read, in the light of cold reason a generation after the close of the war of 1914, the history of the tribunals in England which were charged with examining conscientious objectors to military service and of the military authorities to whom some of those objectors were handed over.[19] No one can go through the record without the sense that some of the tribunals deliberately evaded the purposes of the exemption clause; and it is clear that in the administration of punishment for refusal to obey orders there was wanton cruelty, a deliberate pleasure in the infliction of pain, for which no words can be too strong. Nor is that all. The record shows occasions when ministers of the Crown, when responding to questions in the House of Commons, used evasions of a kind which showed a complete contempt for truth,[20] and yet they were supported in their attitude by the majority of the members there. I note, also, at least one occasion when a number of conscientious objectors were taken from England to France for the purpose of execution by the military authorities; and only the accident that Professor Gilbert Murray was able to appeal on their behalf to the Prime Minister prevented the sentence from being carried out.[21] These are worse than the methods of the Inquisition; for, at least, the members of that tribunal believed that they were rescuing their victims from eternal damnation. Those of whom I speak had no excuse save ignorant prejudice and the blindness of passion.

You will see, therefore, why I cannot believe that constitutional

[19] John W. Graham, *Conscription and Conscience* (London: George Allen & Unwin, 1922), Chap. III.

[20] *Ibid.*, p. 209.

[21] *Ibid.* (I record with gratification, in 1947, that both in Great Britain and in the United States conscientious objectors were treated with far greater understanding in the Second than in the First World War.)

expedients alone, however substantial, will prevent the invasion of liberty. They will work just so long as people are determined they shall work, and no longer. They are valuable because, since they have been consecrated by tradition, their invasion tends to arouse, at least in some of us, a prejudice to which we have become habituated. But to keep them active and alive requires a deliberate and purposive effort it is by no means easy to make when the result of doing so conflicts with some other objects keenly desired. That is, I think, capable of a simple demonstration. No class of men is so carefully trained as the judiciary to the habit of a balanced mind. Yet if you examine the observations of judges in cases where their passions are deeply involved you will note how great is the effort they have to make to show tolerance to antagonistic views. Nor do they always succeed. In most of the classic English blasphemy cases, for example, the judge has too often been, either consciously or unconsciously, an additional counsel for the prosecution.[22] In many of the American Espionage Acts cases what chiefly emerges from the summing up of the judge is a desire, at all costs, to see that the prisoner does not secure an acquittal.[23] Recent injunction cases in America show a desire, no doubt unconscious, on the part of the court to lend aid and countenance to a social philosophy of which it happens to approve.

I conclude, therefore, that in general we, as a society, shall not allow the mechanisms of the state to serve the cause of freedom unless we approve the objects at which freedom aims. In a time of crisis, particularly, when the things we hold most dear are threatened, we shall find the desire to throw overboard the habits of tolerance almost irresistible. For those habits are not in nature, which teaches us that opinions we deem evil are fraught with death. They come from our social heritage, and are part of a

[22] See, for example, William H. Wickwar's *The Struggle for the Freedom of the Press, 1819–1832* (London: George Allen and Unwin, 1928) for an account of judicial *mores* in the early nineteenth century; and H. T. Buckle's pamphlet on the Pooley case for similar conduct thirty years later.

[23] Z. C. Chafee's classic discussion in *Free Speech in the United States* is the best account of this unhappy period. The new edition is even more valuable than the first.

process the value of which we must relearn continuously if we are
to preserve it. That is the meaning of the famous maxim that
eternal vigilance is the price of liberty. It is why, also, it becomes
necessary in each age to restate the case for freedom, if it is to be
maintained.

5

There is one other general part of this political aspect of
liberty that I wish to consider before I turn to a different portion
of my theme. I have argued that resistance to the encroachments
of power is essential to freedom because it is the habit of power
continuously to enlarge, if it can, the boundaries of its authority.
Is there any specific rule by which men can be trained to such
resistance? Is there, that is, a way in which the average citizen
of the modern state can be persuaded that it is in his interest to
be vigilant against those who would invade his rights? Can it,
further, be shown that such a temper in the citizen is likely, as
it grows, to confer benefit upon the community as a whole?

Broadly speaking, I think the answer to these questions is in the
affirmative. I hazard the generalization that the more widespread
the distribution of power in the state, the more decentralized its
character, the more likely men are to be zealous for freedom.
That is, of course, a large statement to make. It implies the
thesis that, in terms of historic experience, good government is
always, in the end, both less valuable and less efficient than self-
government. I mean that, in general, rules imposed upon a
society from above for its benefit are less effective to the end that
they seek than rules which have grown naturally from below.
I believe that to be true both of the individual and the group in
society. The full realization of this thesis is, of course, an impossibility, since it would make the uniformities we need in social life
unattainable. But the greater the degree in which we can realize
it, the better for the community to which we belong.

I do not mean to imply that there is any rigid principle which enables us to mark off the lines of demarcation between what is individual and what is social, between what belongs to the group and what belongs to the state, between the sphere of central and the sphere of local government. The only possible approach to that problem is a pragmatic one, as anyone can see who tries to make common sense out of John Stuart Mill's famous attempt, with its list of exceptions [24] by which he reduced it to something like absurdity. Most of us, I think, could draw up lists of governmental areas in which central and local topics could be demarcated without undue disagreement. We should fairly universally say that foreign policy and defence, fiscal technique and commercial regulation, were naturally within the sphere of the central, as public libraries, baths and wash-houses and playing fields were within the sphere of the local, authority. We should agree that crime is a matter for the state, and sin a matter for the churches. We should admit that there must be uniform regulations for marriage and divorce, but that individuals only could make up their minds when, within the regulations, either to marry or divorce.

This, I think, is pretty straightforward. The points I wish to emphasize are different. They are, first, that in the making of public decisions it is desirable that as many persons as possible who are affected by the result should share in reaching it; and, secondly, that whenever the decision to make some rule of conduct a matter of governmental regulation arouses widespread and ardent dissent, the probability is that the case against the decision is stronger than the case in its favour. Let us take each of these points separately.

My first point I may perhaps best make by the statement that all creative authority is essentially federal in character. The purpose for which authority is exercised is the maximum satisfaction of desire. To achieve that end, it is in the long run vital to take account of the wills of those who will be affected by the decision. For, otherwise, their desires are unexplored, and there is substituted for the full experience that should be available the partial

[24] Thereby laying himself open to FitzJames Stephen's crushing attack.

experience, perhaps suffused with a sinister interest, which is able
to influence the legal source of decision. Maximum satisfaction,
in other words, is a function of maximum consultation; and the
greater the degree in which the citizen shares in making the rules
under which he lives, the more likely is his allegiance to those rules
to be free and unfettered. Nor is this all. The process of being
consulted gives him a sense of being significant in the state. It
makes him feel that he is more than the mere recipient of orders.
He realizes that the state exists for his ends and not for its own.
He comes to see that his needs will be met only as he contributes
his instructed judgment to the experience out of which decisions
are compounded. He gains the expectation of being consulted,
the sense that he must form an opinion on public affairs. He
learns to dislike orders which are issued without regard being paid
to his will. He comes to have a sense of frustration when decisions
are made arbitrarily and without an attempt to build them from
the consent of those affected. He learns vigilance about the ways
of power. Those who are trained to that vigilance become the
conscious guardians of liberty.

For they will protest against what they regard as the invasion of
their rights, and tribute will have to be paid to their protest.
In a civilized community, fortunately for ourselves, power is
always on the defensive; and when men are vigilant to expose its
encroachments it is urgent to seek their good opinion. Those
active-minded enough to fight for their rights will, doubtless, be
always in a minority; but they prick the indifferent multitude
into thought and they thus act as the gadflies of liberty. The
handful of American lawyers who protested against the methods
of the Department of Justice in 1920 forced the department's
officials to a change of their ways. The little group of men who, in
season and out of season, have protested that the white man's
burden ought not, in justice, to be borne by the black, have the
awakening of the subject peoples to their credit: what E. D. Morel
did for the Congo, what H. W. Nevinson did for Portuguese
Angola, these are lessons in the service of citizenship to liberty.

And it is the peculiar value of the habit of vigilance that it grows by what it feeds on. To accustom the average man to regard himself as a person who must be consulted is, in the long run, to assure him, through consultation, of satisfaction. For the holders of power are always desirous of finding the convenient routine; and if they are driven by pressure to give the people freedom, they will discover that this is the object they have set before themselves.

Into the institutional pattern which such a federalization of authority requires I cannot here enter.[25] It must suffice to say that it makes totally inadequate the traditional forms even of the democratic state. For the notion that, when the citizen has chosen his representatives for Parliament or his local authority, he can sit back in the comfortable knowledge that his wants are known, his interests safeguarded, has not one jot of evidence to support it. We need, of a certainty, a much more complex scheme. We have not only to provide for a more adequate relationship between Parliament and the administrative process; we have also to integrate the latter with the public it serves on a much ampler scale than any we have hitherto imagined. I have elsewhere tried to show how vital in this context is the device of the advisory committee. Its value both as a check upon bureaucracy and as a means of making decision genuinely representative in character becomes the more clear the wider our experience of its functioning.

But even this is not enough. There will never be liberty in any state where there is an excessive concentration of power at the centre. The need for a wide distribution of authority away from that centre becomes more obvious with the growth of our experience. If the decisions to be made are to satisfy the needs of those affected by them, the latter must have major responsibility for their making. All of our problems are not central problems; and to leave to the central government the decision of questions which affect only a portion of the community is to destroy in that portion the sense of responsibility and the habit of inventiveness.

25 Cf. my *Grammar of Politics,* Chap. VII.

The inhabitants of any given area need a consciousness of common purposes, a sense of the needs of their neighbourhood, which only they can fully know. They then find that the power to satisfy these needs by themselves gives to them a quality of vigour far greater in the happiness it produces than would be the case if satisfaction were always provided or controlled from without. For administration from without always lacks the vitalizing ability to be responsive to local opinion; it misses shades and expressions of thought and want which it is urgent for successful government to recognize. It lacks the genius of place. It does not elicit creative support from those over whom it rules. It makes for mechanical uniformity, an effort to apply similar rules to unsimilar things. It is too distant from the thing to be done to awaken interest from those concerned in the process of doing it. Centralized government in local matters may be more efficient than a decentralized system; but that superior efficiency will never, as Mill long ago pointed out, compensate for an inferior interest in the result.

I believe, therefore, that, the area of local government, with all its difficulties and dangers, should be as little circumscribed as possible. The German system before 1933 of laying down what a local authority may not do, and leaving it free to experiment outside that realm of prohibition, seems to me superior both in principle and result to its Anglo-American antithesis. Thereby we gain not only the knowledge which comes from varied social experiment, but the freedom of a citizenship trained in the widest degree to think for itself and to solve its own problems. Most imposed solutions of a uniform character succeed only where their material is genuinely uniform. That is rarely the case in matters of local government. And even the impatient reformer ought sometimes to think whether, say, forcing a child-labour law on Georgia by federal amendment will lead to a genuine and whole-hearted application of its terms; whether, in fact, it will not persuade people to hatred of the law, even contempt for the law, by encouraging evasion of it. Successful legislation is almost always legislation for which the minds of men are anxious; the channels of assent to it can rarely be dug too deep.

All that I am saying of territorial locality, moreover, seems to me to apply, with far more emphasis, to what may be termed functional areas also. Everyone acquainted with the history of churches realizes the necessity of leaving them free to develop their own internal life. On matters like ecclesiastical government, dogma, ceremonial, interference by the state is almost invariably disastrous in its results. What is true of churches is true also, *mutatis mutandis,* of other associations. Bodies like the legal and medical professions are much better able to direct their own internal life than is the state. It is necessary, of course, to prevent them from developing into monopolies; and to that end it is essential to devise a framework of principle within which they must work, to retain, also, the right to its revision from without from time to time. But that said, few would, I think, deny that what we call professional standards, the jealousy for the honour of the profession, the sense of *esprit de corps,* the realization that its members owe to the community something more than the qualities for which payment can be exacted, these things are born of the large degree of freedom to define their own life which the professions enjoy.

It is, I think, important to extend that notion of self-government beyond the professions. We ought to learn to think of industries like cotton and coal as entities not less real than Lancashire or New York, as capable, therefore, of being organized for the purpose of government. Most of the plans current today for national economic councils are not, in my judgment, of great value; the problem of satisfactory weighting of the different elements is really insoluble, and any problem that concerns industry as a whole seems to me to be civic in its nature and, therefore, the proper province of the legislative assembly of the state.[26] But these considerations do not apply to industries taken individually, or linked together at special points of intimate contact. It does not seem to

[26] Cf. my *Grammar of Politics,* pp. 82 f.

me inconceivable that we should create a parliament for the mining industry, in which government, management, labour, and the consumer should each have their due representation, and to which should be confided the determination of industrial standards, on the model of professional self-government. I should give to this parliament a delegate power of legislation which would enable it to frame rules of conduct binding upon all the members of the industry. Thus, while Georgia might refuse to pass a child-labour law, a particular industry in Georgia might refuse to allow its members to engage child labour in field or factory. There might be developed in this way a body of industrial legislation and jurisprudence growing naturally out of the experience of those who participate in the operation of the industry, and imposed with a real sense of freedom because it has been developed from within and is not the outcome of an external control. The help this system would give to the creatively minded employer, on the one hand, and to the adventurous trade union, on the other, needs no emphasis from me. The experiments of the Amalgamated Clothing Workers and the Baltimore and Ohio Railroad have amply demonstrated something of what it might effect, if planned in a wholesale way. They show clearly, I venture to suggest, that an authority born of consent is always definitely superior to an authority born of coercion. And the reason is the simple but vital one that creative energy is liberated only in the atmosphere of freedom.

6

In all that I have so far said there is implied a theory of the nature of law upon which, perhaps, I ought to say a word. The view I am taking suggests that law is not simply a body of commands justifiable by virtue of their origin. Laws are rules seeking to satisfy human desires. They are the more certain of acceptance the more fully they seek to inquire what desires it is urgent to satisfy, and the best way of inquiry is to associate men with each stage of the process of lawmaking. For men, in fact, will not obey law which goes counter to what they regard as fundamental. Their notion of what is fundamental may be wrong, or unwise, or limited; but it is their notion, and they do not feel free unless they can act by their own moral certainties. It is useless to tell them that an assumption on their part that they are entitled to forego obedience will result in anarchy. Every generation contains examples of men who, in the context of ultimate experience, deliberately decide that an anarchy in which they seek to maintain some principle is preferable to an order in which that principle must be surrendered. The South in 1861, Ulster in 1914, the Communist in the context of a capitalist society, these are but variations on the great theme of Luther's classic *Ich kann nicht anders.* They illustrate the inescapable truth that law must make its way to acceptance through the channel of consenting minds.

Let me put this in a different way. Law is not merely a command; it is also an appeal. It is a search for the embodiment of my experience in the rule it imposes. The best way, therefore, to make that search creative is to consult me, who can alone fully report what my experience is. There can be no guarantee that law will be accepted save in the degree that this is done. Legal right is made as the individual recipient of a command invests it with right; he gives it his sanction by relating it successfully to his own experience. When that relation cannot be made, the authority of law is always in doubt. And it is in doubt because, by contradicting the experience of those whom it seeks to control, it seems to them a frustration of their personalities. To accept the control would be to become unfree.

An extreme way of putting this view would be to say that law is made by the individual's acceptance of it, that the essence of the lawmaking process is the consent of interested minds. At points of marginal significance, that is, I think, true; and the consequences of the truth are obviously important. Authority, if my view is right, is always acting at its peril. It lives not by its power to command but by its power to convince. And consent is born of conviction for the simple reason that the real field of social action is in the individual mind. Somewhere, inevitably, the power to coerce that mind to ways of thought of which it does not approve breaks down; man, as Father Tyrrell said, is driven on "to follow the dominant influence of his life even if it should break the heart of all the world." That is the stark fact which conditions the loyalty any authority seeks to secure. At some point it cannot be imposed but must be won from us. And the greater the degree in which it springs from that persuasion, the greater, also, is the success of authority in imposing its solutions. No power can ever hope for successful permanence, no power, either, is entitled to it, which does not make its way, in vital matters, through the channels of consent.

From this two conclusions seems to me to flow. Ours is not a universe in which the principles of a unified experience are unfolded. It is a multiverse, embodying an ultimate variety of experiences, never identical, and always differently interpreted. There is enough similarity of view to enable us, if we have patience and goodwill, to make enough unity to achieve order and peace. But that similarity is not identity. It does not entitle us to affirm that one man's experience can be taken as the representation of another's. It does not justify the inference that I shall find what I most truly desire in the desire of another. I am not a part of some great symphony in which I realize myself only as an incident in the *motif* of the whole. I am unique, I am separate, I am myself; out of my own qualities I must build my own principles of action. These are mine only, and cannot be made for me, at least creatively, by others. For their authority as principles comes from the fact that I recognize them as mine. Into them, as principles, I pour my personality, and life, for me, derives its meaning from their unique texture. To accept the forcible imposition upon me of other principles, which I do not recognize as the expression of my experience, is to make of me, who might be free, a slave. I become an instrument of alien purposes, devoted to an end which denies my selfhood. Law, therefore, as coercion, is always an invasion of personality, an abridgment of the moral stature of those whom it invades.

To be true to its purpose, it must reduce the imperative element to a minimum if it is to release creativeness and not destroy it.

The individual, therefore, is entitled to act upon the judgment of his conscience in public affairs. He is entitled to assume that he will not necessarily find the rules of the conduct he ought to pursue objectified in any institution or set of institutions. I agree that, for most of us, conscience is a poor guide. It is perverse, it is foolish, the little knowledge it has is small alongside the worth of the social tradition. But perverse, foolish, ignorant, it is the only guide we have. Perverse, foolish, ignorant, it is at least ours; and our freedom comes from acting upon its demands. We ought, doubtless, to convince ourselves that the path it indicates is one we have no alternative but to follow. We ought to seek the best possible means for its instruction and enlightenment. We should remember that civilization is, at best, a fragile thing, and that to embark upon a challenge to order is to threaten what little security it has. It may even be wise, as T. H. Green once put it, to assume that we should approach the state in fear and trembling, remembering constantly the high mission with which it is charged.

All this may be true, and yet it seems to me to leave the individual no option but to follow conscience as the guide to civic action. To do otherwise is to betray freedom. Those who accept commands they know to be wrong make it easier for wrong commands to be accepted. Those who are silent in the presence of injustice are in fact part-authors of it. It is to be remembered that even a decision to acquiesce is a decision, that what shapes the substance of authority is what it encounters. If it meets always with obedience, sooner or later it will assume its own infallibility. When that moment comes, whatever its declared purpose, the good that authority will seek will be its own good and not the good of those involved in its operations. Liberty means being faithful to oneself, and it is maintained by the courage to resist. This, and this only, gives life to the safeguards of liberty; and this only is the clue to the preservation of genuine integrity in the individual life.

If it is objected that this is a doctrine of contingent anarchy, that it admits the right of men to rebellion, my answer is that the accusation is true. But is its truth important? Order, surely, is not the supreme good, and rebellion has not always been wrong. Power is not conferred upon men for the sake of power, but to enable them to achieve ends which win happiness for each of us. If what the authorities do is a denial of the purpose they serve; if, as we meet their acts, there appears in them an absence of goodwill, a blindness to experience alien from their own, an incapacity imaginatively to meet the wants of others, what alternatives have we save a challenge to power or a sacrifice of the purposes of our lives? We do not condemn Washington because there came a moment in his career when he was compelled to recognize that the time for compromise with England had passed. We do not, even more notably, condemn those early Christians who refused to offer incense to the gods. We have to act by the dictates of our conscience, knowing, as Washington knew, as the early Christians recognized, that the penalties of failure are terrible. But we can so act, also, knowing that there is a sense in which no man who serves his conscience ever fails.

For by that service he becomes a free man, and his freedom is a condition of other men's freedom. There is immense significance in the fact that those who fought for religious liberty were the unconscious progenitors of civil liberty also. When they demanded the right to worship the God they knew, in their own minds they were insisting that in one sphere, at least, of human experience, their own perception must count as ultimate. They consecrated freedom to the service of God. But that, after all, is only one aspect of freedom. Its consecration to the service of man is, for some of us, not less vital and pervasive. To fight for the assurance that a man may do his duty as he conceives it is to fight not only for freedom, but for all the ends which the emancipation of mankind seeks to attain. I do not know whether liberty is the highest objective we can serve. I do assert that no other great purpose is possible of achievement save in the terms of fellowship with freedom.

II. FREEDOM OF THE MIND

1

I HAVE sought, so far, to show that, however important be the political mechanisms on which liberty depends, they will not work of themselves. They depend for their creativeness upon the presence in any given society of a determination to make them work. The knowledge that an invasion of liberty will always meet with resistance from men determined upon its repulsion, this, in the last analysis, is the only true safeguard that we have. It means, I have admitted, that a certain penumbra of contingent anarchy always confronts the state; but I have argued that this is entirely desirable since the secret of liberty is always, in the end, the courage to resist.

The most important aspect of a free atmosphere is undoubtedly freedom of the mind. The citizen seeks for happiness, and the state, for him, is an institution which exists to make his happiness possible. He judges it, I have urged, by its capacity to respond to the needs he infers from the experience he encounters. That experience, I have insisted, is private to himself. Its predominant quality is its uniqueness. Either it is his own, or it is nothing. The substitution for it of someone else's experience, however much wider or wiser than his, is, where it is based upon constraint, a denial of freedom. What the citizen quite rightly expects from the state is to have his experience counted in the making of policy, and to have it counted as he, and he only, expresses its import.

Obviously enough, if his experience is to count, a man must be able to state it freely. The right to speak it, to print it, to seek in

72

concert with others its translation into the event, is fundamental
to liberty. If he is driven, in this realm, to silence and inactivity,
he becomes a dumb and inarticulate creature whose personality is
neglected in the making of policy. Without freedom of the mind
and of association a man has no means of self-protection in our
social order. He may speak wrongly or foolishly; he may associate
with others for purposes that are abhorrent to the majority of
men. Yet a denial of his right to do these things is a denial of his
happiness. Thereby he becomes an instrument of other people's
ends, not himself an end. That is the essential condition of the
perversion of power. Once we inhibit freedom of speech, we inhibit
criticism of social institutions. The only opinions of which serious
account is then taken are the opinions which coincide with the will
of those in authority. Silence is taken for consent; and the decisions
that are registered as law reflect, not the total needs of the society,
but the powerful needs which have been able to make themselves
felt at the source of power. Historically, the road to tyranny has
always lain through a denial of freedom in this realm.

I desire here to maintain a twofold thesis. I shall seek to show,
first, that liberty of thought and association—the two things are
inextricably intertwined—is good in itself; and second, that its
denial is always a means to the preservation of some special and
usually sinister interest which cannot maintain itself in an atmosphere of freedom. I shall then discuss what restrictions, if any, must
be placed upon this right, and the conditions it demands for its
maximum realization. I shall, in particular, maintain that all restrictions upon freedom of expression upon the grounds that they
are seditious or blasphemous are contrary to the well-being of
society.

The case for the view that freedom of thought and speech is a
good in itself is fairly easy to make. If it is the business of those
who exercise authority in the state to satisfy the wants of those
over whom they rule, it is plain that they should be informed of
those wants; and obviously they cannot be truly informed about
them unless the mass of men are free to report their experience.

No state, for instance, could rightly legislate about the hours of labour if only business men were free to offer their opinions upon industrial conditions. We could not develop an adequate law of divorce if only those happily married were entitled to express opinions upon its terms. Law must take account of the totality of experience, and this can only be known to it as that experience is unfettered in its opportunity of expression.

Most people are prepared to agree with this view when it is made as a general statement; most people, also, recoil from it when its implications are made fully known. For it implies not only the right to sanctify the present social order, but the right also to condemn it with vigour and completeness. A man may say that England or America will never be genuinely democratic unless equality of income is established there; that equality of income may never be established except by force; that, accordingly, the way to a genuine democracy lies through a bloody revolution. Or he may argue that eternal truth is the sole possession of the Roman Catholic Church; that men can be persuaded to understand this only by the methods of the Inquisition; that, therefore, the re-establishment of the Inquisition is in the highest interest of society. To most of us, these views will seem utterly abhorrent. Yet they represent the generalizations of an experience that someone has felt. They point to needs which are seeking satisfaction, and the society gains nothing by prohibiting their expression.

For no one really ceases to be a revolutionary Communist or a passionate Roman Catholic by being forbidden to be either of these. His conviction that society is rotten at its base is only the more ardently held, his search for alternative ways of expressing his conviction becomes only the more feverish as a result of suppression. Terror does not alter opinion. On the one hand it reinforces it, on the other it makes the substance of opinion a matter of interest to many who would, otherwise, have had no interest whatever in it. When the United States Customs Department suppressed *Candide* on the ground that it was an obscene book, it merely stimulated the perverse curiosity of thousands to whom *Candide* would have remained less than a name. When the British government prosecuted the Communists for sedition in 1925 the daily reports of the trial, the editorial discussion of its result, made the principles of communism known to innumerable readers who would never, under other circumstances, have troubled to acquaint themselves with its nature. No state can suppress the human impulse of curiosity, and there is always a special delight, a kind of psychological scarcity value, in knowledge of the forbidden. No technique of suppression has so far been discovered which does not have the effect of giving wider currency to the thing suppressed than can be attained in any other fashion.

But this is only the beginning of the case for freedom of speech. The heresies we may suppress today may be the orthodoxies of tomorrow. New truth begins always in a minority of one; it must be someone's perception before it becomes a general perception. The world gains nothing from a refusal to entertain the possibility that a new idea may be true. Nor can we pick and choose among our suppressions with any prospect of success. It would, indeed, be hardly beyond the mark to affirm that a list of the opinions condemned in the past as wrong or dangerous would be a list of the commonplaces of our time. Most people can see that Nero and Diocletian accomplished nothing by their persecution of Christianity. But every argument against their attitude is an argument also against a similar attitude in other persons. Upon what grounds can we infer prospective gain from persecution of opinion? If the view held is untrue, experience shows that conviction of its untruth is largely a matter of time; it does not come because authority announces that it is untrue. If the view is true in part only, the separation of truth and falsehood is accomplished most successfully in a free intellectual competition, a process of dissociation by rational criticism, in which those who hold the false opinion are driven to defend their position on rational grounds. If, again, the view held is wholly true, nothing whatever is gained by preventing its expression. Whether it relates to property or marriage, to religion or the form of the state, by being true it demands a

corresponding change in individual outlook and social organization. For untrue opinions do not permanently work. They impede
discovery and they diminish happiness. They enable, of course,
those to whom they are profitable to benefit by their maintenance,
but it is at the cost of society as a whole.

There is the further question, moreover, of the persons to whom
the task of selecting what should be suppressed is to be confided.
What qualifications are they to possess for their task? What tests
are they to apply from which the desirability of suppression is to
be inferred? A mere zeal for the well-being of society is an utterly
inadequate qualification; for most persons who have played the
part of censor have possessed this and have yet been utterly unfit for their task. The self-appointed person, Mr. Comstock, for
instance, merely identifies his private view of moral right with the
ultimate principles of ethics; and only the intellectually blind
would ask that the citizen be fitted to his vicious bed of Procrustes.
The official censor, a man like the famous Pobedonostsev,[1] normally assumes that any thorough criticism of the existing social
order is dangerous and destructive; and thereby he transforms
what might be creative demand into secret attack, which is ten
times more dangerous in its influence. If you take almost any of the
men who have been appointed to work of this kind, you discover
that association with it seems necessarily to unfit them for their
task. For it turns them into men who see undesirability in work
which the average man reads without even a suspicion that it is
not the result of experience with which he ought to be acquainted.
Anyone who looks through the list of publications prohibited by
the Dominion of Canada will, I think, get a sense that the office of
censorship is the avenue to folly.[2] No one with whom I am acquainted seems wise enough or good enough to control the intellectual nutrition of the human mind.

What tests, further, are there to apply? Broadly speaking, we

[1] Konstantin Pobedonostsev (1827–1907), Russian jurist, advocate of an extreme policy of censorship.
[2] A list is printed in Morris Ernst and William Seagle, *To the Pure* (New
York: The Viking Press, 1928), pp. 296–302.

suppress publications on the ground that they are obscene or dangerous. But no one has ever arrived at a working definition of obscenity, even for legal purposes. Take, for instance, two books suppressed by the English magistrates for obscenity in 1929. One, Miss Radclyffe Hall's *Well of Loneliness,* seemed to men like Mr. Arnold Bennett and Mr. Bernard Shaw a work which treated a theme of high importance to society in a sober and high-minded way. They saw no reason to suppose that the treatment of its difficult subject—sexual perversion—could be regarded by any normal person as offensive. The magistrate, Sir Chartres Biron, took a different view. I, certainly, am not prepared, on *a priori* grounds, to say that a lawyer, however well trained in the law, has a better sense of what is likely to produce moral depravity than Mr. Bennett or Mr. Shaw; and a reading of Miss Hall's dull and sincere book only reinforces that impression. Another book was distributed privately and secretly—Mr. D. H. Lawrence's *Lady Chatterley's Lover*—in a limited and expensive special edition. I gather that its public sale would have been definitely prohibited. Yet I observe that some of the most eminent American critics have praised it as the finest example of a novel seeking the truth about the sexual relations of men and women that an Englishman has published in the twentieth century. That may be—I am not competent to say—excessive praise. My point is that in a choice, say, between the average police magistrate and Mr. Robert Morss Lovett, I am not prepared to accept the former's opinion of what I may be safely left to read.

Let me remind you, moreover, of what cannot too often be pointed out, that the rigorous application of the legal tests of obscenity would prohibit the circulation of a very considerable part of the great literature of the world. The Bible, Shakespeare, Rabelais, Plato, Horace, Catullus, to take names at random, would all come under the ban. It is worth while pointing out that those most concerned with the suppression of "obscene" books are religious people. On their tests of obscenity the Bible certainly could not hope to escape; yet they believe, in general, that the Bible is the inspired word of God, a position which, I venture to suggest, should at the least give them pause. I do not know, indeed, how we are to create a healthy social attitude to the problems of sex, if all that deals with it from a new point of view, and with a frankness that admits the experimental nature of our contemporary solutions, is to be dismissed as obscene. Questions like those of birth control, extramarital love, companionate marriage, sexual perversion, cannot really be faced in a scientific fashion by applying to them the standards of a nomadic Eastern people which drew up its rules more than two thousand years ago. Virtuous people who shrink from frank discussion in this realm seem to me probably responsible for more gratuitous suffering than any other group of human beings. The thing they call "innocence" I believe to be quite wanton ignorance, and, by their abridgment of freedom, they imprison human personality in a fashion that is quite unpardonable.

The same seems to me to be the case in the realm that is called blasphemy. I have no sort of sympathy with that attitude of mind which finds satisfaction in wanton insult to the religious convictions of others. But I am not prepared for its suppression. For I note that, historically, there are no limits to the ideas which religious persons will denounce as blasphemous; and, especially, that in an age of comparative religious indifference, the hand of persecution almost invariably chooses to fall only on humble men.[3] It attacks Mr. G. W. Foote, the secularist, but it leaves Lord Morley free to do infinitely more damage than any for which Mr. Foote can ever have been responsible. I cannot, moreover, forget that what is blasphemy in Tennessee is common sense in New York, that the works of Wollaston and Toland and Chubb, which seemed entirely blasphemous to their generation, seem commonplace to us. Every religious body really means by blasphemy an attack upon its fundamental principles. Such attacks are, of course, necessarily circulated to bring those principles into contempt.

---

[3] This is brought out well in Gerald D. Nokes's excellent book, *A History of the Crime of Blasphemy* (London: Sweet and Maxwell, 1928).

We who read Paine's *Age of Reason* with admiration for its cogency of argument, its trenchant style, its fearless appetite for truth, can hardly avoid a sense of dismay when we remember the days when it was secretly passed from hand to hand as an outrageous production, the possession of which was itself an indication of social indecency.

And here let me remind you of certain facts on the other side. We denominate as blasphemous works calculated to bring the principles of Christianity into hatred, ridicule, or contempt. As I have said, I entirely dislike the type of work which finds pleasure in offensiveness to Christians. But if we are to suppress works and punish their authors because they cause grief to certain of our fellow-citizens, exactly how far are we to carry the principle? A very large part of propagandist religious literature is highly offensive to sincere and serious-minded persons who are unable, in their consciences, to subscribe to any particular creed. When you remember the descriptions applied by Mr. William Sunday to those who do not accept Christianity, you cannot, I think, avoid a sense that there is a religious blasphemy for which, at least from the angle of good manners, nothing whatever can be said. Mr. Sunday is only one of the worse offenders in a whole tribe of preachers and writers by whom belief, however sincere, that is alien from their own is normally and naturally described in language it is a euphemism to call Billingsgate; and they bring charges of immorality against unbelievers for which not an atom of proof exists. Are we to suppress all such expressions also? And if we are to continue this campaign of prohibition to its appointed and logical end, shall we have time for any other social adventure?

Nor is this all. In the world of education we are continually presented with the problem of textbooks which are offensive to a particular denomination. We are asked, for instance, to prohibit their use in schools. I once sat as an appointed member of the Education Committee of the London County Council. I was presented there with a requisition, drawn up by a Catholic body, against the use of certain books on the ground that they contained

untrue statements about questions like the Reformation, in which
Catholics are particularly interested. But I have not observed in
the same Catholic body a desire to use in their own denominational
schools only those textbooks which Protestants are prepared to
accept as a true picture of the Reformation. Nor is this problem
of school textbooks merely religious in character. Americans of
our own generation have seen passionate controversy over the
views of the War of Independence, of the Constitution, of the
motives and responsibility in the war of 1914, which are to be
presented not merely to school children, but also to university
students; there is a heresy-hunt in the fields of politics and economics, a desire to have only "true" opinions taught to the
immature mind. But "true" opinions, on examination, usually
turn out to be the opinions which suit the proponents of some
particular cause. In London we used to think that a "true" theory
of value was best obtained from the works of Professor Cannan; in
Cambridge they pinned their faith to Marshall and Pigou; in the
Labour Colleges ultimate wisdom was embodied in the writings of
Marx, and Cannan, Marshall, and Pigou were all dismissed as the
pathetic servants of bourgeois capitalism. Is anything gained for
anyone by insisting that truth resides on one side only of a particular mountain range? Is it not wisdom to begin by an admission
of its many-sidedness? And does not that admission involve an
unlimited freedom of expression in the interpretation of facts?
For facts, as William James said, are not born free and equal. They
have to be interpreted in the light of our experience; and to limit
this interpretation is to suppress someone's personality, to impose
upon him our view of what his life implies to the forcible exclusion of that in which alone he can find meaning. I can see neither
wisdom nor virtue in action of this kind.

So far, I have restricted my discussion to the nonpolitical field,
and before I enter the political area I want, for a moment, both
to summarize the position we have reached and to admit the one
limitation on freedom of expression I am prepared to concede.
I have denied that prohibitions arising from blasphemy or

obscenity, or historical or social unfairness, have any justification.
They seem to me unworkable. They are bad because they prevent
necessary social ventilation. They are bad because they exclude the
general public from access to facts and ideas which are often of
vital importance. They are bad because no one is wise or virtuous
enough to stand in judgment upon what another man is to think
or say or write. They are bad because they are incapable of
common-sense application; there is never any possibility of a wise
discrimination in their application. They give excessive protection to old traditions; they make excessively difficult the entrance
of new. They confer power in a realm where qualifications for
the exercise of power, and tests for its application, are, almost
necessarily, nonexistent. For the decision on every question of this
kind is a matter of opinion in which there is no prospect of
certainty. Suppression here means not the prohibition of the
untrue or the unjust or the immoral, but the prohibition of
opinions unpleasing to those who exercise the censorship. Historically, no evidence exists to suggest that it has ever been exercised for other ends.

I do not see any rational alternative to this view. But here I
should emphasize my own belief that, broadly speaking, such
freedom of expression as I have discussed means freedom to
express one's ideas on general subjects, on themes of public
importance, rather than on the characters of particular persons.
I have not, I think, a right to suggest that Jones beats his wife, or
that Brown continually cheats his employer, unless I can prove,
first, that the suggestions are true, and second, that they have a
definite public importance. I have not the right to create scandal
because I find pleasure or profit in speaking ill of my neighbour.
But if Brown, for instance, is a candidate for public office, my
view that he cheats his employer is directly relevant to the question
of his fitness to be elected; and if I can prove that my view is true,
it is in the public interest that I should make it known. I cannot,
that is to say, regard my freedom of expression as unlimited. I
ought not to be permitted to inflict unnecessary pain on any

person unless a proportionate gain to social welfare results from that infliction.

On the other hand, I would make one remark here that seems to me of increasing importance in a society like our own. The public interest in the habits of individuals is real, and we must be careful to give it its proper protection. It is, I think, reasonable to doubt whether the Anglo-American law of libel, in its present state, does not push too far the right of the individual citizen to be protected from comment. Outrageous damages, which bear no measurable relation to anything, are often claimed and not seldom awarded. Where a political flavour enters into a case, it is difficult, and sometimes impossible, to persuade a jury to consider the issue on its merits. I have myself sat on a jury in a political libel case of which I can only say that I was almost persuaded, by the habits there displayed, to doubt the validity of the jury system altogether. I am tempted to suggest that, criminal libel apart, it would be worth while considering the abolition of damages in all political or quasi-political cases, and the concentration, as an alternative, upon proper publicity for the form of apology where the libel is held to be proved. We have, for instance, got into the bad habit in England of thinking that the social position of the plaintiff is a measure of the damages he should receive; and it is well known that there are places where, for instance, a Socialist could hardly hope even for a favorable verdict from any average jury. The case for careful inquiry, at any rate, seems to me to be made out. As the law at present stands and works, I do not think I could even say of a candidate for the House of Commons that he is not likely to be more than a permanent back-bencher without having to pay heavily for my opinion.

2

But I turn from these relatively simple matters to the political aspect of freedom of expression, which is, of course, the pith of the whole problem. How far is a man entitled to go in an attack upon the social order? What opinions, if any, are to be prohibited on the ground that they incite to subversive conduct? Is there a distinction between the printed word and the spoken word? Is there a distinction between speech in one place and speech in another? Is there a difference between normal times and a time of crisis like, let us say, a war or a general strike? At what point, if any, do words become acts of which authority must take account to fulfil its primary duty of maintaining the peace?

It will, I think, be universally agreed that all criticism of social institutions is a matter of degree. Let us take the problem first as we meet it in normal times, and let us view it from the angle of the English law of sedition.[4] Here it may be said at once that were the literal terms of that law enforced, political controversy in England would be impossible. For the declared purpose of the law is to prevent the established institutions of the state from being brought into hatred or contempt, and every leader of the opposition is seeking to do precisely that when he makes a political speech. Anyone who reads, for instance, the utterances of Lord Carson at the time of the Home Rule fight in 1914, or even of Mr. Ramsay MacDonald in the General Election of 1929, cannot avoid the conclusion that, taken literally, they were seditious. Yet all of us agree that it is not the purpose of the law to prevent such speeches being made. When, therefore, if ever, is that law to be brought into operation?

We must, I think, begin with a distinction between the written and the spoken word. If an English Communist leader writes a book or pamphlet, whatever its substance, and to whomever it is addressed, I do not think the law ought to be used against him save in an instance where deliberate defamation of a person has proved to be untrue, or where an attack upon a group like Jews or Negroes is intended to incite to action through the evocation of hate. For it is the history of these matters that if governments once begin to prohibit men from seeking to prove in writing that violent revolution is desirable, they will, sooner or later, prohibit

[4] 53 Geo. III, c. 160.

them from saying that the social order they represent is not divine. In Italy under Mussolini, for example, papers were actually suppressed not for anything positive that they said, but because there was absent from their pages frequent and emphatic eulogy of his regime; there were even calls for suppression because particular papers, while saying no word against Mussolini, had been too insistently eulogistic of the Papacy before the Concordat. I yield to no one in my dissent from large sections of Lenin's analysis of the nature of the modern state. But I think it urgent that his criticism should be available to society. For it represents the impress made upon him by the experience of political life, and a government which remains unaware of that criticism has lost its chance of seeking to satisfy the critic. If it begins by assuming that the exposition of revolutionary communism is undesirable, it will end, as the record shows, by insisting that language classes to teach English to Russians are a form of Communist propaganda. There is never any such certitude in matters of social constitution as to justify us in saying that any exposition of principles must be suppressed. No authority has ever a capacity for wise discrimination in these matters; and, even if it had, I do not see why it is justified in the exercise of discrimination.

For suppression, in the first place, as I have said, never permanently convinces. What it does is to drive a small body of men to desperation and to reduce the masses to complete apathy in political matters. Most men who are prohibited from thinking as their experience teaches them soon cease to think at all. Men who cease to think cease also in any genuine sense to be citizens. They become the mere inert recipients of orders which they obey without scrutiny of any kind. And their inertia induces in the government that false confidence which mistakes silence for consent; that is, perhaps, the most vital lesson of Hitlerism. The government which is not criticized at its base never truly knows the sentiments to which its activity gives rise among its subjects. It must ultimately fail to satisfy them because it does not know what desires it has to satisfy. Political thought, after all, however unwise or mistaken, is never born in a vacuum. Lenin's view of capitalist society is just as relevant to its habits as the view of the Duke of Northumberland or of Judge Gary; each is born of contact with it, and each, as it is expressed, has lessons to teach from which, as these are scrutinized, a wise policy can be born.

Here, I think, it is relevant to say a word upon one special aspect of freedom of expression for printed matter. I have argued that no limit, save two, of any kind should be placed upon it, at any rate in normal times. The book, the pamphlet, and the newspaper ought to circulate with unimpeded freedom in whatever direction they can move. Many people who sympathize with this view will, however, except from this freedom printed material which is addressed to the armed forces of the state; and most governments, of course, have special legislation, with especially severe penalties, against any attempt at interference with the loyalty of the military services. I cannot myself see that this exception is justified. The armed forces of the state consist of citizens. The government has quite exceptional opportunities to retain their allegiance. If a printed document is able to sow disaffection amongst them, there must be something very wrong with the government. And, in fact, whenever agitation has produced military or naval disloyalty, it has been the outcome not of affection for the principles upon which the agitators laid emphasis, but of grievances which have made either soldiers or sailors responsive to a plea for their disloyalty. That was the case with the Spithead mutinies of 1797; with the French troops in 1789; with the Russian troops in 1917. If the army or the navy is prepared to turn upon the government, the likelihood is great that the government is unfit to retain power. For anyone who can disturb the allegiance of a mind as trained to obedience as that of the soldier or the sailor has, I believe, an *a priori* case for insisting that his particular philosophy corresponds to an urgent human need.

It is said that ideas are explosive and dangerous. To allow them such unfettered freedom is, in fact, to invite disorder. But to this position there are at least two final answers. It is impossible to draw a line round dangerous ideas, and any attempt at their definition involves monstrous folly. If views, moreover, which imply possible disorder are able to disturb the foundations of the state, there is something supremely wrong with the governance of that state. For disorder is not a habit of mankind. We cling so eagerly to our accustomed ways that, as even Burke insisted, popular violence is always the outcome of a deep popular sense of wrong. The common man can be persuaded to revolt, granted his general habits, only when the government of the state has lost its hold upon his affections; and that loss is always the reflection of a profound moral cause. We may, indeed, go further and argue that the best index to the quality of a state is the degree in which it is able to permit free criticism of itself. For this ability implies an alertness to public opinion, a desire to remedy grievance, which enables the state to gain ground in the allegiance of its citizens. Almost always freedom of speech results in a mitigation which renders disorder unnecessary; almost always, also, prohibition of that freedom merely makes the agitation more dangerous because it drives it underground. Rousseau was infinitely more dangerous as a persecuted wanderer, because infinitely more interesting and, therefore, infinitely more persuasive, than he would have been if left unfettered in Paris. Lenin did far more harm to Russia as an exile in Switzerland than he could ever have accomplished as an opposition leader in the Duma. The right freely to publish the written word provides, in fact, the supreme catharsis of discontent. Governments that are wise can always learn more from the criticism of their opponents than they can hope to discover in the eulogies of their friends. When they stifle that criticism, they prepare the way for their own destruction.

There is, I think, an undeniable difference between freedom of written expression and freedom of spoken expression. In the one case, a man attempts conviction by individual persuasion; he seeks, by argument which he believes to be rational, to move the minds of those who read what he has written. To speak at a meeting raises different problems. No one with experience of a great crowd under the sway of a skilled orator can doubt the speaker's power deliberately to create disorder if he so desires. A speaker at Trafalgar Square, for instance, who urged a vast meeting of angry unemployed to march on Downing Street, could do so with a fair assurance that they would obey his behest. I do not think a government can be left to the not always tender mercies of an orator with a grievance to exploit. The state, clearly, has the right to protection against the kind of public utterance which is bound to result in disorder.

But no government is itself entitled to assume that disorder is imminent: the proof must be offered to an independent authority. And the proof so offered must be evidence that the utterance to which the government takes exception was, at the time and in the circumstances in which it was made, definitely calculated to result in a breach of the peace. The government's prohibitions must not be preventive prohibitions. It must not prohibit a meeting before it is held on the ground that the speaker is likely to preach sedition there. It must not seek conviction for sedition where the utterance might, under other circumstances, have resulted in a breach of the peace. To use my earlier illustration, I think a government would be justified in prosecuting the Trafalgar Square orator; but I do not think it would be entitled to prosecute the same speaker if he made the same speech on Calton Hill in Edinburgh. For we know that when men in Edinburgh are incited to march on London, they have a habit of turning back at Derby. I conclude, therefore, that the test adopted by Mr. Justice Holmes, in his deservedly famous dissent in *Abrams* v. *U.S.*,[5] is the maximum prohibition a government can be permitted. If it is in fact demonstrable that the speech made had a direct tendency to incite immediate disorder, the punishment of the accused is justified. I think such cases should always be tried before a jury. Experience suggests that a random sample of popular opinions is more likely to do justice in this type of case than is a judge. I have myself

[5] *Ut supra.*

been present at such trials before a magistrate, where the whole
case for the prosecution quite obviously broke down and where,
nevertheless, a conviction was secured. I do not for a moment
suggest that we can be confident that a jury will act wisely; but
my sense of our experience is that there is less chance of its acting
unwisely than in the case of persons who occupy an official position
of any kind. With the best will in the world, officials tend to be
unduly responsive to executive opinion.

You will see that my desire is to maximize the difficulties of any
government which desires to initiate prosecutions in this realm.
My reason for this view is the quite simple one that I do not trust
the executive power to act wisely in the presence of any threat,
or assumed threat, to public order. Anyone who studies the treason
trials of 1794, or, which are even more striking, the cases under
the Espionage Act in America during 1917–1920, will be convinced
of the unwisdom of allowing the executive an undue latitude.
Every state contains innumerable stupid men who see in unconventional thought the imminent destruction of social peace. They
become ministers; and they are quite capable of thinking that a
society of Tolstoyan anarchists is about to attempt a new gun-
powder plot. If you think of men like Lord Eldon, like Sir William
Joynson-Hicks, like Attorney General Mitchell Palmer, you will
realize how natural it is for them to believe that the proper place
for Thoreau or Tolstoy, for William Morris or Mr. Bernard Shaw,
is a prison. I am unable to take that view; and I am therefore
anxious that they should not be able to make it prevail without
hindrance.

                                    3

Views such as I have put forward are often regarded with
sympathy when their validity is limited to normal times. In a
crisis, it is argued, different considerations prevail. When the
safety of a state is threatened, it is bound to take, and is justified
in taking, all action to end the crisis. To suggest that it should

then be bound by principles which weaken its effective striking power, is, it is said, to ask it to fight with one hand tied behind its back. The first objective of any society must be organized security; it is only when this has been obtained that freedom of speech is within the pale of discussion.

I am unable to share this view. We have really to examine two quite different positions. There is, first, the question of the principles to be applied in a period of internal violence; there is, next, the quite special question of limitation upon utterance in a period of war. I agree at once that it is entirely academic to demand freedom of speech in a time of civil war, for the simple reason that no one will pay the slightest attention to the demand. Violence and freedom are, *a priori,* contradictory terms. But I would point out two things. In general, revolutions fail in their major creative purposes because those who make them deny freedom to their opponents. Losing criticism, they do not know the limits within which they can safely operate; they lose their power because they are not told when they are abusing it. I can think of no period in history when a revolutionary government has gained by stifling the opinion of men who did not see eye to eye with it; and I suggest that the revolutionary insistence that persuasion is futile finds little creative evidence in its support.

But when once the question has been settled of who is to possess power, other questions of urgent delicacy arise in which, as I think, the principles I have laid down possess an irresistible force. There is the problem of how the rebels and the disaffected are to be treated; of whether the resumption of order is to be followed by free discussion; of the power to be exercised by the military authority over ordinary citizens not engaged in armed hostility to the regime. Here I can only express the view that the resumption of order ought always to be followed swiftly by the establishment of normal principles of judicial control; and that the military authorities ought not, save where it is quite impossible for the civil courts to exercise their jurisdiction, to have any power over ordinary citizens.

These are rigorous views; and perhaps I may devote a little time to their exposition. I know of no case where the state has exercised extraordinary power outside the normal process of law in which that power has not been grossly abused.[6] It was abused in the American Civil War, even by a mind so humane and generous as that of Lincoln; it was emphatically and dangerously abused in the Amritsar rebellion of 1919. Let me illustrate, from this latter example, some of the abuses that may occur. Two men were arrested in Amritsar, prior to the declaration of martial law, and deported to a remote and undisturbed part of the province; on the declaration of martial law, they were brought back to Lahore, which was in the martial law area, and tried and sentenced by a martial law tribunal. A number of pleaders were arrested in Gudaspur, where there was no disturbance, taken under revolting conditions to Lahore, and confined there in the common jail for a period lasting up to a month. They were then released, without any charges being preferred against them; on the evidence, indeed, it is difficult to know with what offence they could have been charged. Again, in the trial of one Harkishan Lal, and others, for treason and waging war against the King-Emperor, the accused were not allowed to have a lawyer of their own choosing; a full record of the case was not taken, and the private notes of counsel for the defence had to be surrendered by him to the court at the end of each day. It is difficult to see how, under such conditions, any adequate defence was possible. Again, a punitive detachment, under a Colonel Jacob, tried by drumhead court-martial, and flogged, a man who refused, it appears with some truculence, to say who had destroyed some telegraph wires; later it appeared that the man, as he had asserted, had in fact no knowledge of who had destroyed them. In Lahore—to take a final instance—the military officer in command prohibited the congregation of more than a

---

[6] The war of 1939 has provided a notable exception to this judgment of 1930. The special powers conferred upon the Churchill government in the spring of 1940 were used in the domestic field, for nearly five years, with great imaginative wisdom by Mr. Herbert Morrison. On the other hand, up to the surrender of 1940, the French government used its special powers badly; and the treatment of the Nisei by the American government is a tragic story.

few persons in the streets; a few persons did so congregate and they were flogged. On investigation, after the flogging, it was found that the group was a wedding-party whose purpose was not more dangerous than that of any other persons engaged in a similar function.[7]

I do not, of course, suggest that there is anything especially cruel or remarkable in these instances. Whether you study repression in Ireland or Russia, Bavaria or Hungary or India, its history is always the same. The fact always emerges that once the operation of justice is transferred from the ordinary courts to some branch of the executive, abuses always occur. The proper protection of the individual is deliberately neglected in the belief that a reign of terror will minimize disaffection. There is no evidence that it does. If it could, there would have been no Russian Revolution, and there would have been no movement for Indian self-government. The error inherent in any invasion of individuality, such as a system of special courts implies, is that it blinds the eyes of government to the facts not only by suppressing expression of opinion, but by persuading government that most opinion which finds expression is illegitimate if it is not in the nature of eulogy. Even Lincoln supported his generals in completely indefensible attacks on civilian rights. Executive justice, in fact, is simply a euphemism for the denial of justice; and the restoration of order at this cost involves dangers of which the price is costly indeed.

The problem of war is, in a sense, a special case of the problem of disorder; but in fact it raises quite different considerations. Let me first of all make the point that if you are a citizen in a besieged town, you cannot expect a normal freedom of speech; to be within the area of actual military operations means that you must not hope to be regarded as an individual. You become, from the nature of things, a unit of attack or defence whose personality is immaterial and insignificant. The position here is extraordinary; and principles have little or no relation to the problems that arise. The case, as elsewhere, merely affords proof that liberty and

[7] Cf. my *Grammar of Politics,* p. 554.

violence are antithetic terms. This was the British position in 1940.

But let us rather take the position of a citizen whose country is involved in war as, say, England in 1914, or America in 1917, was involved. What are his rights and duties then? I would begin by making the point that the fact of belligerency does not suspend his citizenship; he owes as much, perhaps more than ever, the contribution his instructed judgment can make to the public good. The scale of operations cannot, I think, make any difference to that duty. It is as real, and as compelling, when the scale is big, as in the war of 1914 or that of 1939, as when, as in the Boer War or the Spanish-American War, the scale is relatively small. If I think the war a just one, it is my duty to support it, and if I think it unjust there is no alternative open to me except opposition to it. I believe, for instance, that the opposition of Mr. Eugene Debs or Mr. Philip Snowden to the war of 1914 was a fulfilment, on their part, of the highest civic obligation. No citizen can assume that his duty in wartime is so to abdicate the exercise of his judgment that the executive has a blank cheque to act as it pleases. No government, therefore, is entitled to penalize opinion at a time when it is more than ever urgent to perform the task of citizenship. If a man sincerely thinks, like James Russell Lowell, that war is merely an alias for murder, it is his duty to say so even if his pronouncement is inconvenient to the government of the day.

I cannot, indeed, believe that there is any case on the other side worthy of serious consideration. In the war of 1914 it was said that hostile opinion must be controlled because it hindered the successful prosecution of the war. But behind the façade of prejudice implied in the use of a term like hostility, there are several issues, each one of which requires analysis. For what does "hostile opinion" mean? Does it imply hostility to the inception of a war, to the methods of its prosecution, to the end at which it aims, to the terms on which its conclusion is proposed? In the war of 1914, the critics were divided into camps on each of these views. There were men, like Mr. Snowden, who thought the war unjustified in its inception and bad in its conclusion. There were others who criticized the manner, both diplomatic and technical, of its prosecution. Was it, for instance, hostility to the prosecution of that war to criticize Lord Jellicoe's conduct at the Battle of Jutland, or Sir Ian Hamilton's handling of the operations at the Dardanelles? Was it, again, hostility on the part of *The Times* to attack the Asquith Government on the ground, rightly or wrongly, that it showed a lack of energy in building up a munitions supply? If a statesman not in office, like Mr. Theodore Roosevelt in 1916, thinks the diplomatic policy of the executive likely to be attended by fatal results, must he confine himself to private representations, lest public utterance hinder the national unity? If a statesman believes, as Lord Lansdowne did and as President Wilson believed in 1916, that peace by negotiation is preferable to peace by victory in the field, because of the human cost that victory entails, has he no obligation to his fellow-citizens who are paying that cost with their lives?

It is evident from our experience that to limit the expression of opinion in wartime to opinion which does not hinder the war's prosecution is, in fact, to give the executive an entirely free hand, whatever its policy, and to assume that, while the armies are in the field, an absolute moral moratorium is imperative. That is, surely, a quite impossible position. No one who has watched at all carefully the process of governance in time of war can doubt that bona fide criticism was never more necessary. Its limitation is, in fact, an assurance that mistakes will be made and wrong done. For once the right to criticize is withdrawn, the executive commits all the natural follies of dictatorship. It assumes a semi-divine character for its acts. It deprives the people of information essential to a proper judgment of its policy. It misrepresents the situation it confronts by that art of propaganda which, as Mr. Francis Cornford has happily said, enables it to deceive its friends without deceiving its enemies. A people in wartime is always blind to the facts of its position and anxious to believe only agreeable news; the government takes care to provide it only with news that is pleasant. If no such news is at hand, it will be manufactured. Petty successes

will be magnified into resounding victories; defeats will be mini-
mized wherever possible. The agony of the troops will be obscured
by clouds of censorship. A wartime government is always obtuse
to suggestion, angry when inquiry is proposed, careless of truth.
It can, in fact, only be moralized to the degree to which it is
subject to critical examination in every aspect of its policy. And
to penalize the critic, therefore, is not only to poison the moral
foundations of the state, but to make it extremely difficult, when
peace comes, for both government and the mass of citizens to
resume the habits of normal decency.

Freedom of speech in wartime, therefore, seems to me broadly
to involve the same rights as freedom of speech in peace. It involves
them, indeed, more fully, because a period of national trial is one
when, above all, it is the duty of citizens to bear witness. I do not,
of course, mean that a citizen in wartime should be free to com-
municate secret military plans to the enemy; I do mean that
if a man feels, like Sir Henry Campbell-Bannerman, that British
policy in South Africa uses "methods of barbarism," it is his right,
as well as his duty, to say so. Obviously critical activity of this kind
will be unpopular, and a government which helps in the making
of its unpopularity will find the task of suppression easy. But it
will pay a heavy price for suppression. The winged words of
criticism scatter, only too often, the seeds of peace. Sir Henry
Campbell-Bannerman's attack on the Balfour Government persuaded General Botha that trust in Great Britain might not
be misplaced; President Wilson's speeches, especially his Fourteen Points, were by implication a criticism of Allied policy,
and they awakened liberal opinion in Germany to a sense of its
responsibilities. Wartime unity of outlook, in a word, is never
worth the cost of prohibitions. If the policy of a state which decides
upon war does not command the general assent of its citizens, the
state has no right to make war. If the number of those hostile is
considerable, the policy is, at the least, a dubious one. If the
number is small, there is no need to attempt suppression in the
interest of success. The only way, in fact, to attain the right is by

free discussion; and a period of crisis, when the perception of right is difficult, only makes the emphasis upon freedom more necessary.

Let me illustrate my view with reference to one or two of the decisive factors in the Peace of Versailles. No one now believes the wartime lie that Germany alone was responsible for the war of 1914; her responsibility may be greater than that of some others, but it is agreed that the burden of Russia is at least as heavy and that war, in any case, was rooted in the nature of the European system. But, in the interest of Allied unity, it was regarded in the Allied countries as essential to represent Germany as the sole conspirator against European peace. She was painted as a malefactor whose sins were incapable of exaggeration. Her virtues were denied, her achievements belittled, until what Mr. Walter Lippmann terms a "stereotype" of her was built up for public use which made her appear to the average man a criminal who could not be too severely punished. The statesmen who constructed this stereotype knew that it was untrue; but they hoped, doubtless, to escape its consequences when the victory had been won. They found that they could not do so. They had so successfully repressed all effort at reasonable delineation that the atmosphere of hate was unconquerable. They had no alternative to a Carthaginian peace because that seemed, to the masses they had deceived, the only possible course for justice to take. They knew, as, for instance, the famous memorandum of Mr. Lloyd George made manifest,[8] that a Carthaginian peace would be disastrous for Europe; but it was too late to destroy the legend they had created. Like those whom Dante describes in the *Inferno,* they were punished by the realization of their announced desires.

The world, in this context, has paid the price for the suppression of truth; and another phase of the suppression should also be remembered. It is usually agreed that some of the worst elements in the Peace of Versailles were the result of the secret treaties by which the Allies, exclusive of America, bound themselves to each

[8] Cd. 1614 (1922).

other before the entrance of America into the war. Nowhere among
the associated powers was the desire for a just peace more widespread than in America; nowhere, also, was the discussion of war
aims more rigorously curtailed as a hindrance to the full prosecution of the war. Had discussion of the peace been full and effective
in the critical war years, the liberal instincts of President Wilson
might, when reinforced by the weight of informed opinion, have
compelled at least a considerable mitigation of the secret treaties.
They had been published in the American press after their dis-
closure by the Bolsheviks in 1917; full discussion would have
revealed their inadequacies and enabled the President to counter-
act what there was of evil in their substance. But the destruction of
free opinion prevented revelation of these inadequacies, and Mr.
Wilson did not seriously give his mind to them until he reached
Paris. It was then too late to undo their consequences. Here in fact,
as elsewhere, uncontrolled power acted to blot out the only atmosphere in which truth could have been made manifest. No government was compelled to do its duty, because the means were want-
ing to inform it of what its duty was. The powers had forgotten, or
had chosen to forget, that they could not attain a just peace save
by freeing the minds of men and women who cared for justice.

4

So far, I have considered freedom in the political sphere as
though it concerned only a single individual as opposed to society
and the state. I have sought to discuss what his freedom means in
the complex relationships in which he is involved. But obviously
this is an undue simplification of the problem. The individual, in
fact, does not stand alone; he joins hands with others of like mind
to persuade, sometimes to compel, society to the adoption of the
view they share. It is unnecessary for me to emphasize the vital part
played by associations in the modern community.[9] Granted that
they have their dangers, they are not only a vital expression of

[9] Cf. my *Grammar of Politics*, pp. 256 ff.

human personality, but an expression as natural as the state itself. That a man must be free to combine with his fellows for joint action in some realm in which they have a kindred interest is, I take it, of the essence of liberty. The point it is important to examine is the degree of control, if any, that the state is entitled to exercise over voluntary associations.

Let me say at once that I know no question more difficult in the whole range of political science. I am quite certain that, from the angle of individual freedom, the less interference the state attempts, the better for everyone concerned; but, equally, it is clear that the state is fully entitled to some interference. I should deny, for instance, the right of any voluntary association to inflict physical punishment or imprisonment upon its members; and I should argue that any state was justified in immediate and drastic interference to prevent such infliction. But the real problems we encounter are not so simple as this. Joseph Smith announces his reception of a message from Heaven ordaining the duty of men to practise polygamy in a community where the law recognizes only monogamy; what rights of interference has the state when a body of men and women join him and begin to give effect to his teaching? What are the rights of the state when a congress of trade unionists declares a general strike? Are those rights different when the purpose of the strike is industrial from what they are if it is political? How are we to distinguish between the two? What are the rights of combination among men employed in industries the nature of which makes the service they perform fundamental to the community? What should be the attitude of the state to a society of men engaged in propaganda for a revolution by the use of physical force? Is there a difference between such a society when it merely preaches the desirability of such a revolution and when it acts to that end? Does action, in the latter case, mean embarkation upon rebellion—for example, the purchase of machine-guns —or does it extend, say, to the stirring up of industrial strife in the hope that a resort to political rebellion may be its outcome?

You will see that these are not merely academic questions; every

one of them has been in the forefront of political discussion in
this last half-century, and all save the first have been vital themes
of decision in the years since 1914. Let us take first the case of an
association which, like the Mormon Church, desires to practise
modes of conduct different from those pursued by the society as a
whole. We have to assume that the members of the association have
joined it voluntarily, and continue voluntarily in its membership.
We have to assume, further, that they do not desire to force their
particular way of life upon others; for some single realm of conduct, like the realm of marriage, they desire that they shall be left
free from interference by the organized power of society. I cannot
see that we are entitled to interfere with them. We may think them
unwise, foolish, muddle-headed, immoral. We know perfectly well
that we cannot hope, by the external constraint of law, to abolish
all conduct that comes within those terms. I happen to think that
it is a gross superstition to leave money to the Roman Catholic
Church that masses may be said for the testator's soul; but I should
think it an unwarrantable interference with the relations between
that Church and its members if such bequests were forbidden. I see
no evidence to suggest that the practice of polygamy is worse, in
its nature, than a hundred other practices which organized society
either directly permits or wisely leaves alone because it knows that
rigorous control would be utterly futile. The only way to deal with
the ideals of the Mormon Church is to prove their undesirability
to their members. On the evidence of history, persecution will not
be acceptable as proof; and it is not improbable that the only legal
effect of prohibition has been to make furtive and dishonest what
was, at first, open and avowed. This seems to me the case with all
similar problems of association. If a society of women, enthusiastic
for the independence of their sex, formed themselves into an association to propagate and practise the (to them) ideal of having
children outside the tie of marriage, I should not think the state
entitled to interfere with its work. So, too, I should argue, with a
principle like birth control. The state is not entitled to prohibit
diffusion of such knowledge, or the use of it. When it does, it makes

the family nothing more than an instrument of fecundity, and destroys the whole character of that right to privacy which is the foundation of harmonious sexual relationship.

I argue, therefore, that voluntary bodies are entitled, outside the realm where their ideas and conduct are intended directly to alter the law or to arrest the continuity of general social habits, to believe what they please and to practise what they please. This would not permit a body of burglars to take over from Proudhon the principle that property is theft and assume the right to restore it to themselves; but it would justify, to take the case of principles I personally abhor, a society of Mormons practising polygamy in a society like that of the United States.

Let me turn from this to the political field. I take first the question of the right of the state to control freedom of association in the industrial sphere. Practically speaking, the question reduces itself to one of whether the state is justified in limiting the power of a trade union, or of a combination of trade unions, to call out its members on strike. I want to put on one side the technical juristic questions involved and to discover, if I can, the justice of the general arguments which underlie the problem.

These are, I think, broadly four in number. It is argued that the state has a right to prohibit a general strike on the ground that this is an attempt to coerce the government, either directly, by making it introduce legislation which it would not otherwise initiate, or indirectly, by inflicting such hardship on the community that public opinion forces the government to act. It is said, secondly, that the state is entitled to prohibit those whom it directly employs, for example postmen, from either going on strike or affiliating themselves with any organization the nature of which may compromise the neutrality of the government. It is said, thirdly, that certain industries, railways, for example, or electricity supply, are so vital to the community that continuity of service in them is the law of their being, and that, therefore, the right to strike can be legitimately denied to those engaged in them. It is argued, fourthly, that a limitation upon the purposes of trade

unions, so that they are confined within their proper industrial
sphere, is also justified.

I want to analyse each of these principles separately, but certain
preliminary observations are important. In any industrial society,
as Mr. Justice Holmes has insisted,[10] liberty of contract always
begins where equality of bargaining power begins. Granted, therefore, the normal conditions of modern business enterprise, only
the existence of strong trade unions will ensure to the average
worker just terms in his contract of service. If he stands alone, he
has neither the knowledge nor the power to secure for himself
proper protection. Nor is this all. Strong trade unionism always
means that public opinion can be made effective in an industrial
dispute. One has only to compare the situation in the British
textile industries, where, if there is a dispute, the power of the
unions compels the state to search for terms of a just settlement,
with that in America, where, because of the weakness of the unions,
the state seems hardly to know when a dispute has occurred, where,
also, the police power is almost invariably exerted on the side of
the employer, to realize the meaning of strong trade unionism. It
is, in fact, the condition of industrial justice. No limitation upon
freedom to associate is, I urge, permissible unless it can be demonstrated that clear and decisive advantage to the community, includ-
ing, be it remembered, trade unionists themselves, is likely to
result.

In this background, let us examine the first of the four principles
I have enumerated. It is argued that no coercion of the government, direct or indirect, is legitimate. If men want to obtain from
government a solution which government is not willing to attempt,
the way to that end is not by the use of industrial power, but
through the ballot-box at a general election. Or, from the angle
of indirect coercion, it is pointed out that the first interest of the
state is in the general well-being of the community; a general strike
necessarily aims at that well-being and may therefore be prohibited. The general strike, even a large sympathetic strike, is in

10 *Coppage* v. *Kansas*, 236 U.S. 1.

fact a revolutionary weapon. As such, it is a threat to the Constitution and illegal as well as unjustifiable.

I do not think the problem is so straightforward as the delusive simplicity of this argument would seem to make it. If it is said that the Trades Union Congress of Great Britain would not be justified in calling a general strike to compel the government to make Great Britain a federation, I should agree at once. But I point out that no one supposes it would take such action and that therefore a prohibition of it is unnecessary. But I should not agree that a general strike is unjustified to secure the eight-hour day, or to protect the payment of unemployment relief, or to continue the Trade Board system—which safeguards labor against sweatshops—in sweated industries. Whether a general strike for these or similar ends would be wise is another matter. I am not prepared to say that it cannot be justified until I know the circumstances of some given case. I am not willing, for instance, to condemn the General Strike of 1926; on a careful analysis of its history, I believe that the blame for its inception lies wholly at the door of the Baldwin Government. No one acquainted with the character of the trade-union movement but knows that a weapon so tremendous as the general strike will be called into play only on the supreme occasion. To lay it down as law that, whatever the occasion, the weapon shall not be used, seems to me an unjustifiable interference with freedom.

I am not greatly moved by the argument that it involves coercion of the government. There are occasions when that coercion is necessary, and even essential. I believe that was the case in Great Britain in 1926. The trade unions would never have called the strike had they seen in the policy of the government even the fragment of a genuine search for justice. But the fact was that Mr. Baldwin and his colleagues simply acted as the mouthpiece of the mine owners. To illegalize a general strike in that background is to say that the trade unions should have acquiesced in the defeat of the miners without an attempt to prove their solidarity with them. It would establish the idea that the ultimate weapon of labour is one which the government need never fear.

There is no danger that the general strike will ever be other than a weapon of the last resort; the occasions when it can be successfully used will be of the utmost rarity. But they may occur. I cannot accept the position that government is always entitled to count on industrial peace, whatever its policy. Nor do I see why it is unconstitutional for labour to withdraw from work in an orderly and coherent way, as it did in 1926.

I do not deny, of course, that both a general strike and others of far less amplitude inflict grave injury and hardship upon the community. But when trade unions seek for what they regard as justice, one of their most powerful sources of strength is the awakening of the slow and inert public to a sense of the position. Effectively to do this, in a real world, the unions must inconvenience the public; that awkward giant has no sense of its obligations until it is made uncomfortable. When it is aroused—if, for instance, trains do not run or coal is not mined—the public begins to have an interest in the position, to call for action. Without some alternative which attempts to secure attention for a just result— and I know of no such alternative—the infliction of hardship on the community seems to me the sole way, even if an unfortunate way, to the end the trade unions have in view. To limit the right to strike is to impose a form of industrial servitude. It means, ultimately, that the worker must labour on the employer's terms lest the public be inconvenienced. I can see no justice in such a denial of freedom.

Two further points it is worth while to make. It is sometimes agreed that while the state ought not to restrict freedom of association for industrial ends, it is justified in doing so when the strike weapon is used for some political purpose. This, indeed, was one of the objectives of the Baldwin Government in enacting the Trades Disputes Act of 1927. But I know of no formula whereby such a division of purposes can be successfully made. There is no hard and fast line between industrial action and political action. There is no hard and fast line which enables us to say, for instance, that pressure for a factory act is industrial action, but pressure for the ratification of the Washington Hours Convention political. Extreme cases are easy to define; but there is a vast middle ground with which the trade unions must concern themselves, and this escapes definition of a kind that will not hamper the trade union in legitimate activity vital to its purpose. And there are certain types of political action by trade unions—a strike against war, for example—which I do not think ought, in the interest of the community itself, to be abandoned. Quite frankly, I should have liked to see a general strike proclaimed against the outbreak of war in 1914; and I conceive the power to act in that way as a necessary and wise protection of a people against a government which proposes such adventures. You cannot compartmentalize life, and where grave emergencies arise the weapons to be utilized must be fitted to meet them. A government which knew that, when it intended aggressive action, its declaration of war was likely to involve a general strike, would be far less likely to think in belligerent terms. I do not see why such a weapon should be struck from the community's hand. I do not forget that the German Republic was saved from the Kapp Putsch by a general strike.

Nor must we forget the limits within which effective legal action is possible. *Jus est quod jussum est* is a maxim the validity of which is singularly unimpressive. When the issue in dispute seems to the trade unions so vital that only by a general strike can they defend their position adequately, they will defend their position, whatever the law may be. Legal prohibition will merely exacerbate the dispute. It will transfer the emphasis to legality, which serves merely to conceal the dispute's true nature. A legal command is, after all, a mere static form of words; what gives it appropriateness is its relevance as just to the situation to which it is applied. And its relevance as just is determined not by those who announce that it is to be applied, but by those who receive its application. The secret of avoiding general strikes does not lie in their prohibition but in the achievement of conditions which render them unnecessary.

Nor is the denial of the right to declare a general strike nec-

essarily a protection of the total interest of the community. Right
and wrong in these matters must be defined in each particular
case. A government which meets the threat of a general strike is
not entitled to public support merely because it meets the threat.
It is no more possible to take that view than it is to say that all
governments deserve support when they confront a rebellion of
their subjects. Everything depends on what the general strike aims
at; everything depends on the purpose of the rebellion; and the
individual trade unionist must make up his mind about the one,
just as the individual citizen must make up his mind about the
other. Law in this realm is, in fact, largely futile. It could not
prevent a general strike by men who saw no alternative open to
them; and it would merely intensify the rigours of such a strike
when it came. The limitation of liberty in this realm seems to me,
therefore, neither just in its purpose nor beneficent in its results.

I do not, of course, deny that freedom of action in this field
is capable of being abused. That is the nature of liberty. Any body
of persons who exercise power may abuse that power. It is an
abuse of power when an employer dismisses his workmen because
he does not like their political opinions. It was an abuse of power
when the owners of halls in Boston refused to rent them to the
promoters of a meeting in memory of Sacco and Vanzetti. It was
an abuse of power when British naval officers connived at the
attempted internment of the Belgian Socialist, M. Camille
Huysmans, in England. It was, I think, an abuse of power when
the Universities of Oxford and Cambridge refused to admit
Nonconformists as students, and when Parliament refused to seat
Mr. Charles Bradlaugh because he was an infidel. But the trade
unions are no more likely, on the historic record, to abuse their
power than is Parliament itself. The latter has the legal competence
to abolish the trade unions if it wished, to disenfranchise the working classes, to confine membership of the House of Commons to
persons with independent incomes. We know that Parliament
is unlikely to do any of these things because omnicompetence
when gravely abused ceases to be omnicompetent. And the same

truth holds, it seems to me, in respect to the liberty to proclaim a general strike.

A much more difficult problem arises where the second of the four arguments is concerned. A government is, I think, entitled generally to the loyal and continuous service of its employees. It is therefore entitled to make regulations which restrain their liberty of action. The army, the navy, and the police, in particular, occupy a special position in the state; if they were free, like ordinary citizens, to withdraw their labour as they pleased, the executive power would be in an impossible position. The government, therefore, may make suitable regulations for the control of these services. But it is important that, in the framing of these regulations, care should be taken that the conditions of service are just. To be just, two principles are, I suggest, of primary importance. The regulations should be made and administered .in conjunction with those who are affected by them; and in their application or change executive action should not be the final court of appeal. The principles which we in England call Whitleyism [11] are the *quid pro quo* which government servants of this type are entitled to expect in return for the surrender of the right to strike; and Whitleyism must include the right of those servants to appeal from an executive decision to such a body as the Civil Service Division of the Industrial Court. To leave the executive sole master of the field is to invite the kind of purblind folly which resulted, in 1919, in the police strikes of Boston and London. Here, certainly, the fact that the governments concerned were the judges in their own cause made it impossible for the police to get either attention or justice without drastic action. And I wish to draw attention to the fact that although in each case the original strikers were defeated, their successors obtained the terms, and even more than the terms, for which they fought.

The defence forces of the state constitute a special case. When

[11] From the name of J. H. Whitley, a system of councils of representative employers and workers for the discussion of industrial relations.

we turn to the ordinary public services, central and local, quite different considerations emerge. If you analyse the British government, for instance, you will find a very small body of men and women who may be regarded as concerned with the making of policy; below them is another body, perhaps two or three times as large, engaged in assembling the material out of which policy is made, and applying it in minor cases; while below these is a vast army of clerks engaged in routine work of a more or less mechanical kind. It cannot, I think, be said that to this last class government emerges as an employer different in kind from what they would encounter in the ordinary labour market. General economic conditions govern their pay; in France and America, indeed, their salaries are below, rather than above, the level obtaining elsewhere for their kind of work. All their interests go along with those of people engaged in similar employment outside the sphere of government activity. Their union, therefore, with persons in private firms seems to me justified in order to raise their general economic level; and I do not see the justice of prohibiting it as was done by the Baldwin Government in the Trades Disputes Act of 1927. (This injustice was remedied by its repeal in 1945 by Mr. Attlee's government.) I think, further, that they are entitled to strike, if they believe there is no other way in which they can secure the enforcement of their demands; though I think, also, that the executive would be justified in compelling them to exhaust the resources of a comprehensive scheme of conciliation before they went so far. The history, indeed, of most modern civil services (France being a notable exception) [12] shows clearly that there is no danger of officials abusing the right to strike. But it shows also the unwisdom of leaving the government free to determine the substance of the contract of service. The government is just as likely as any private employer to extract the most it can get for the least it needs to give; and it is no more fit than any other employer to be left

[12] Cf. my *Authority in the Modern State* (New Haven: Yale University Press, 1919), Chap. V.

uncontrolled in this field. The more labour conditions in government service are determined by an independent authority, the more reasonable they are likely to be. We must not be led away by false claims to a special majesty born of its sovereign character to regard the state as entitled to a peculiar and uncontrolled power over its servants. History shows that the state is just as likely as anyone else to abuse an unlimited authority.

The civil servant is not merely an employee of government; he is also a citizen. In our own day, especially, delicate questions have arisen as to the right of the civil servant, or of a person engaged in the armed forces of the state, to enjoy all the normal political privileges of a person in private employ. Is a civil servant, for instance, entitled to enter on a political career with the chance, if it is interrupted, to return to his department? Most modern states, England, for instance, and Canada, and South Africa, regard political activities as beyond the area within which a civil servant may engage. France, on the other hand, hardly limits its officials in this way, and the Weimar Republic expressly allowed its officials to engage in politics, and some fifty civil servants were at one time in the Reichstag, with the power to return to their departments if they were defeated. Certainly there are few rights for which the rank and file of officials press so strongly as for this; and they regard the limitation of their political opportunities as an invasion of civil liberty at once unnecessary and unjustifiable.

I do not think the problem is a simple one; and I therefore think any solution of it must be complex in character. If a high official of the Foreign Office in England could be elected to Parliament, spend a term there in bitter criticism of the Foreign Secretary, and then, on defeat, return to work with the minister whom he had sought to destroy, the latter's position would, I think, be intolerable. There is, that is to say, a class of civil service work the very nature and associations of which involve exclusion from political life; and if those engaged therein desire political careers, they must terminate their connexion with the civil service. We can, of course, draw a line. I see no reason why all the industrial employees of the government—postmen, for instance, or shipwrights in a national dockyard—should not enjoy all ordinary civil rights. I see no reason, either, to expect any deleterious consequences if civil servants below what we in England call the executive are allowed ordinary political rights, so long as a decent discretion in their exercise is observed. Those engaged in the making of policy must, in my judgment, accept a self-denying role in this regard. Unless government can be assured that its chief civil servants are aloof from political ties, it cannot trust them; and all the considerations which create a "spoils system" will then come into play. Since experience makes it evident that a spoils system is incompatible with either honest or efficient administration, a restriction upon the liberty of public officials is, I would argue, justified. It is an inevitable part of their contract of service, from the point of view of the end that service is intended to secure.

I believe, further, that this restriction applies with special force to the army and navy and to the police. The state is justified, in the interest of the community, in placing an absolute embargo upon the political activities of all members of these services. For unless this activity is restrained, their allegiance becomes the possession of a party and they cannot give that neutral service which is the basic principle of their existence. Anyone who remembers the attempted use of the British Army in 1913 and 1914 on behalf of Ulster, the habits of the French Army during the Dreyfus period, the peculiar relations between the German Army and the monarchy, will easily see how vital is this abstinence. There are American cities where the relations between big business and the police mean that the authority of the latter is certain to be abused in an industrial dispute. Nothing, perhaps, illustrates more nicely the delicacy of this problem than the activities of Sir Henry Wilson [13] during the years after 1912. He was, it appears,

---

[13] Charles E. Callwell, *Field-Marshal Sir Henry Wilson* (New York: Charles Scribner's Sons, 1927), Vol. II, *passim*.

prepared to go from a meeting of the Committee of Imperial Defence to a discussion of its plans with the leaders of the Conservative opposition, and to advise with them upon the best way of rendering some of those plans nugatory. Even during the war of 1914 he did not cease from the cultivation of political intimacies of this kind. Nor must we forget that Sir John French, when he was Commander-in-Chief of the British armies in France, was ready to go behind the back of the government he served to offer secret information to the military correspondent of a Conservative newspaper; and the result of that betrayal of confidence was the breakdown of the first Asquith Government in 1915. The proper conduct of political life is clearly impossible if the armed forces of the state are free to take a definite part in its formation. No one would endorse the Russian principle that a soldier's quality is a function of his agreement with the political faith of the government; yet once relations are established between the politician and the army a movement towards this principle is inevitable. Sooner or later, under such conditions, the army, like the Praetorian Guard, determines the personality of the state. When that occurs, no one can hope for the enjoyment of political freedom.

I turn, in the third place, to the view that industries which have a vital impact on social life can restrain the right to strike of those engaged in them. That is a doctrine peculiarly favoured at the present time; some writers even use the analogy of the army and navy, and argue that the principles applicable to these have a legitimate extension to other fields. Others—the eminent French jurist M. Léon Duguit, for example—take a similar view, but upon other grounds. They argue that vital public services—transport, for instance, or electricity supply—derive their whole meaning from continuity; to allow an interruption of them is therefore to destroy the whole law of their being.

I am as willing as anyone, I hope, to agree that an interruption of a vital public service is undesirable and that every possible step to minimize the possibility of its occurrence should be taken.

But I do not think the denial of the right to strike obtains this end
in any public service, and I do not believe that the same considerations apply to every sort of vital public service. It must, I think,
make a difference whether the industry is operated primarily for
private profit or not; for only in the latter case is its quality as
both vital and public fully recognized. No one, surely, can
examine the record of the coal industry either in England or in
America and say that the motives which have underlain its ownership by private interest are compatible with the view that
uninterrupted service to the community has been the first object
of the owners. There are several reasons of primary importance
for retaining the right to strike so long as private ownership
continues in this sphere. If, for instance, a steamship company
proposes to send out a ship under the conditions in which the
Vestris of ill-fated memory sailed in the spring of 1929, I think
the crew would be justified in striking in the public interest. So,
also, I should argue that the Seamen's Union would be justified
in striking to see to it, if it could, that every vessel putting to sea
carries wireless equipment. Again, a body of miners might, in
my judgment, justifiably strike if they believe that some part of
a pit is too dangerous to be worked without an alteration of
the physical conditions in that particular place. I should, further,
urge that a strike to secure a national agreement for uniform
conditions in a particular industry as against a variety of local
agreements is a justifiable enterprise if that end could not be
attained in any other way.

My view, broadly, reduces itself to this: Where the vital industry is in public hands, the conditions which should operate
are those which relate to government service in general; where
it is in private hands, the state is, I think, justified in seeing to
it that the danger of dislocation is reduced to a minimum; but
it is not justified in saying that, in the event of a disagreement,
the employees shall always abide by the results of compulsory arbi-
tration. For, first of all, the employees will not always do so; their
refusal, doubtless, will be exceptional, but there will be instances

in which it will occur. The famous munitions strikes on the Clyde, and the South Wales miners' strike, during the 1914 war show that this is the case. It is, I suggest, obvious folly to attempt legislation which cannot be enforced at the critical point of urgency. The business of the state, therefore, is not to prohibit, but to find how best to make the strike the final and not the first instrument in conflict.

This, I suggest, can be accomplished in two ways. It can be done, first, by limiting the profits private ownership can make in any industry of vital importance, either absolutely so that the owners are debenture holders merely, and not the residuary legatees of any profit made, or relatively, as in a scheme like that laid down for the gas companies of London. The state is then, I suggest, legitimately entitled to argue that a curb on the liberty of the employer to make what profit he can justifies a curb on the right to strike by postulating the conditions under which alone that right can become operative. Those conditions are, I think, met by some such instrument as the Canadian Industrial Disputes Investigation Act. Under its terms we should then have, at least, enforced public inquiry into the dispute, and the consideration by both sides, as well as by the general opinion of the community, of a reasoned attempt at a solution of the difficulty. We should respect freedom of association by leaving it at liberty to insist that the proposed solution is unjust, while we should protect the public interest in continuity of service by insisting that the right to strike shall not operate until the resources of conciliation have been exhausted.

I reject, therefore, M. Duguit's notion that public interest in continuity of service is a paramount consideration which should overrule all others; and I see no reason to apply his vituperative adjectives [14] to those who take a different view. It seems to me quite definitely a denial of liberty for which no justification can be found to say that men shall work on terms they think utterly unjust; and the argument that, if they do not like those terms,

[14] *Le Droit Social*, Lect. III.

they can find other work, is increasingly without force in a community like our own. The number of those in any society who have a genuine choice, at any given time, of alternative occupations is notably small. An electrician cannot suddenly become a barrister, as the latter can suddenly become a journalist; and if it is a matter of hundreds, or even thousands, of men, the compulsion upon them to continue in the vocation for which they have been trained is obvious. The community never gains, in the long run, from work performed by men who labour under a sense of injustice. The psychological feeling of frustration is poisonous to a harmonious personality. As such, it is incompatible with that search for freedom which, I have urged, is a condition of happiness. I cannot, therefore, agree that the community is entitled, on any terms, to put its convenience first and the workers' freedom afterwards.

A final problem in this same realm remains. The trade union, it is said, must obviously concern itself with all that touches the industrial conditions of its members. But it is not entitled to a general licence to roam all over the field of public activity. We should resent it if a football club passed resolutions upon the foreign policy of a government; and, it is argued, it is in the same way illegitimate for a trade union to deal with matters outside its sphere. The state, therefore, is entitled to define that sphere and to limit the activities of trade unions to matters that come within it.

But I have already sought to show that such a definition of spheres is, in fact, impossible of achievement. Take, for instance, foreign policy. You cannot say that trade unions ought not to concern themselves with foreign policy, since this is intimately bound up with economic policy, which, in turn, is the chief factor in the determination of the conditions of employment. You cannot exclude any part of the economic realm from the trade-union sphere. I should agree that a trade union ought not to concern itself, let us say, with the question of whether the Pope was justified in making the Immaculate Conception a dogma of the Roman Catholic Church; but the likelihood of a trade union acting in this way is as small as that of a football club concerning itself with foreign policy. We cannot legislate for the exceptional instance. Law can deal only with normal habits susceptible of logical reduction to well-established categories. When it goes further, it merely reveals its own impotence. A trade union, more-over, is a living body; and no law has ever been successful in coping with the growth of living things by legal promulgations upon the fact of growth. Many matters are regarded today as normally and naturally within the sphere of the trade unions which a generation ago, even a decade ago, most men would have insisted were in no wise labour's concern. Let me remind you only that in the Ameri-can garment industry the union concerns itself, as a vital part of its function, with the efficiency of the employers for whom its members work. A generation ago, this would have been dismissed as an insolent interference with the rights of management; today it is obvious that upon no other terms can the function of the trade union be fulfilled. In 1914 the unions would never have deemed it their business to concern themselves with the bank rate and credit policy; today they realize that these matters lie at the heart of their problems. Any Procrustes' bed of definition seems to me, therefore, a quite wanton and foolish interference with freedom.

5

Such a discussion of the relation of trade unionism to the state illustrates, I think, the general problem of the approach to free-dom of association in the political sphere. I have denied the right of the state to control the internal life of associations; and I have sought to show the limits of liberty where that life has ramifica-tions outside the groups themselves. It is, I think, a good general rule that the state should not interfere in this realm unless it must. Whenever, for example, it has interfered with the claims of churches to lead their own lives, conflict has been the inevitable outcome. For, in any meeting of church and state, the latter will assert its paramountcy; and a church has no alternative but to deny that assertion. For this reason I believe that any attempt at partnership between them is bound to result in injury to freedom somewhere. If, as in England, the church is formally established by the state, its dependency becomes obvious as soon as it develops ideas of which the state does not approve; in matters like marriage and divorce and education, the Church of England has had to surrender positions held for centuries to preserve the privileges of establishment. It now appears that where there is disagreement in an established church, the minority, on defeat, will not hesitate to disregard the organs which formally record the voice of the church, in order to maintain doctrine or ritual which the church itself seeks to change; and a legislative assembly most members of which are either alien from the church or without competence in its technical problems will find itself defining the church's most sacred principles. Such a church, quite obviously, is the mere creature of the state; it sacrifices its spiritual birthright for a material mess of pottage. Or, as in the Concordat between Italy and the Papacy, there may be a looser alliance of which the result is to deprive all non-Catholics of their right to a secular state treating all religions equally in the realms of marriage and education. I cannot avoid the conclusion that in this historic realm only the American principle of complete separation and noninterference can produce freedom. Unless state and church pursue independent paths, liberty is sacrificed; for either fusion or partnership will, in fact, involve a conflict for supremacy.

The remaining question I wish to discuss in this context is the right of the state over associations the purpose of which is the overthrow of the existing social order. What powers here ought the state to possess? At what point can it interfere? Has it what may be termed a preventive capacity, a right to prevent the development of associations the natural tendency of which will be an attempt at such overthrow? Or should its jurisdiction be limited to punishment for overt acts? Obviously the quality of liberty depends very largely upon the powers we give the state in this realm. I take it as elementary that the state has a right to protect itself from attack. It must, as a state, assume that its life is worth preserving. It must demand that changes in its organization be the outcome of peaceful persuasion and not the consequence of violent assault. A state must, therefore, assume that its duty to maintain peace and security lies at the very root of its existence. The liberty which associations enjoy must therefore be set in the context that they cannot have the liberty to overthrow the state. To that extent, any denial of freedom to them is justified.

But what are the limits within which that denial must work? The world today is littered with organizations that are denied a legal existence and suppressed at any opportunity. The existence of a Communist party is denied by Lithuanian law; the Peasants' party in Yugoslavia was formally dissolved; Russian principle seems to be imprisonment or exile of members of any organization which can be suspected of counter-revolutionary tendencies. We must, I think, begin with the principle that a government is not entitled to suppress associations the beliefs of which alone are subversive of the established order. For otherwise persecution will be built, not on fact, but on suspicion that facts may one day emerge, not on overt acts, but on principles of faith which are in truth dangerous only when they are expressed in practice. A society might be formed, for instance, to discuss and propagate the principles of Tolstoyan anarchy; I do not think any government has legitimate ground for interference with it. The time for that interference comes only when, outside the specific categories of peaceful persuasion, men have moved to action which cannot logically be interpreted as other than a determination to overthrow the social order.

I agree, for instance, that a society of Communists which began to teach its members military drill could legitimately be regarded as a direct threat to peace. So, also, when a political party, the Ulster Volunteers, for instance, or their opponents, the Nationalists, begins to purchase munitions of war, interference by govern-

ment is justified. But I cannot see that a government is entitled
to prevent a society of Communists from preaching their doctrines
either by speech or by publication of the printed word. It is, I
think, essential that, as with the English law of treason, the
government should be compelled to prove in a court of law the
commission of some overt act which directly tends to imminent
rebellion, and to bring at least two witnesses to bear testimony to
its commission. It ought not to be sufficient for a government to
say that since a particular party has beliefs which include the right
to violence and has elsewhere practised violence, its suppression
is legitimate. When Mr. Gandhi announced that if the British
government did not grant Dominion Home Rule in India by the
end of 1929, he and his followers would practise civil disobedience,
such as a refusal to pay taxes, I do not think that announcement
would have justified the British government in imprisoning Mr.
Gandhi before the end of 1929 in order that he might be prevented
from accomplishing his threat at a later time. Or, once more, Lord
Ponsonby's organization of men pledged to refuse military service
in the event of Great Britain going again to war ought not to
have been suppressed simply because, if Great Britain did go to
war, some hundred thousand individuals would refuse to obey any
military service act that would then be enacted.

I am anxious, as you will see, to make it difficult for the government of a state to attack an organization the views of which it happens to dislike. In the light of the evidence, we can rest assured
that, unless we compel proof in an ordinary court of law that
overt acts have been committed, such attacks will be made. One
has only to remember the British treason trials of 1794, where
there was not a scintilla of evidence against any one of the accused,
or the follies enacted by the government during the trials. In
August of 1929, an Italian official actually drew public attention
to the undue circulation, as he deemed, of books by Chekhov,
Turgenev, and Tolstoy; [15] we can be sure that if a society for the
study of Russian literature had then existed in Italy, the attention

[15] *The Observer*, August 18, 1929.

of the government to its suppression would have been called. In the opening stages of the Communist trial in Meerut, the counsel for the prosecution drew attention not merely to the alleged offences of the accused but also to the actions of the Russian Communist leaders from 1917 to 1920, though it is difficult to see how either Indian or English Communists could have been held responsible for them. The logic, indeed, of habitual government suppression seems to be that abnormal opinion is always dangerous because, if it is acted upon, the supremacy of the law will be endangered. That is, of course, perfectly true. If the Communist party in England sought to initiate a rebellion, there would be a threat to the supremacy of the law. But no one of common sense believes today in a Communist menace in England, least of all, perhaps, the Communists themselves. What can possibly be gained by an attempt to suppress the Communist philosophy by an imprisonment of its adherents is quite beyond my understanding. I see no evidence to suggest that the slightest good has been accomplished in America by all the legislation against criminal syndicalism. Nor can I see that anything would have been gained by the kind of prohibitions which the Lusk Committee, of dubious memory, sought to put on the statute book.

My point is that men are always entitled to form voluntary associations for the expression of grievance and for the propagation of ideas which, as they think, will remedy what they believe to be wrong. They are not entitled to move to the commission of acts which bring them into conflict with the state. By acts I mean things like the planning of Mussolini's march on Rome, or the training of civilians as soldiers by the Ulster Defence Council, or the organization of uniformed gangs of thugs by the British Union of Fascists. Acts like these the government may legitimately attack because they have a clear and direct relation to violence, actual or prospective. But governments would do well to remember what they are too prone to forget, that they do not remove grievance, however ill-conceived, by suppressing it. And if they are allowed to associate violent opinion with actual violence, there are few follies upon which they cannot be persuaded to embark. The persecution of opinion grows by what it feeds on. Every social order is ardently upheld by fanatics who are eager to make dissent from their view a crime. The last thing that is desirable is to give them an opportunity for the exercise of their fanaticism.

It is, further, of great importance that all trials relating to these offences should be held in the ordinary courts under the ordinary forms of law. Experience makes it painfully clear that special tribunals are simply special methods for securing convictions. For the mere creation of a special tribunal persuades the ordinary man that there is an *a priori* case against the accused, that the burden of proof lies upon the accused rather than upon the government. Whatever we can do to safeguard these trials from the introduction of passion is an obligation we owe to liberty. However wrong or unwise we may think the actions of men so accused, we have to remember that they represent, as a general rule, the expression of a deeply felt resentment against social injustice. We have to protect ourselves from protest which seeks deliberately to dissolve the bonds of order. But it is our duty, too, to respect that protest when it is sincerely made. And we cannot, therefore, permit attack upon it because it represents ideas or experience alien from our own. *De nobis fabula narretur* is a maxim which every citizen should recognize as the real lesson of political punishment.

Implied in all this is a view of the place of voluntary associations in the community, the significance of which I do not wish to minimize. I am, in fact, denying that they owe their existence to the state, or that the latter is entitled to prescribe, by means of its agents, the terms upon which they can live. The special place of the state in the great society does not, in my judgment, give it an unlimited right to effect that co-ordination which is its function on any terms it pleases. The principles of a legitimate co-ordination bind the state as much as they bind any other body of men. Each of us finds himself part of a vast organization in the midst of which we must seek the realization of desire. We cannot attain it alone.

We have to find others with kindred desires who will join hands with us to proclaim the urgency of realization. There is no other way to the attainment of our desire; and an attitude, therefore, like that of Rousseau, who denied the legitimacy of any voluntary associations, fails altogether to take account of the elementary facts of social life. Such bodies, indeed, must run in the leading-strings of principle, but the decision as to what that principle must be is not one the state alone is entitled to make. For the latter is not justified in preventing the expression of desire; it is justified only in preventing the realization of desire by violent means. It must tolerate the expression of experience it hates because it is there, as a state, to satisfy even the experience it cannot understand. We must not, in fact, allow ourselves to fall into the error of believing that opinion which is antagonistic to the state's purpose is unworthy to survive. The state's purpose, like any other, is expressed through the agency of men. They may misinterpret it; they may, consciously or unconsciously, pervert it to their own ends. To leave them free to settle the limits of voluntary association would be to leave them free to settle what criticism of their work they were prepared to permit. That is a power which could not safely be entrusted to any body of men who have ever operated as a government.

For consider, once more, the historic record. The Roman suppression of Christianity was built upon the principle that unity of religious belief is the necessary condition of citizenship; later experience shows that view to be without any substance. What in fact emerges from the history of religious persecution is the lesson that the unity made by the suppression of Nonconformity is the unity of stagnation. That was the history of France under the repeal of the Edict of Nantes; it has been the history of Spain ever since the sixteenth century; it is, indeed, the history of any community, however rich and powerful, the rulers of which assume that they know what constitutes truth and right, what opinions, therefore, they are entitled to proscribe. Any government which attacks a body organized to promote some set of opinions which may become dangerous to its safety may fairly be presumed to have something to conceal. It is co-ordinating social life, not to the end of greater fullness, but simply for the sake of co-ordination.

But law, as I have insisted earlier, does not exist for the sake of law. It is not entitled to obedience because it is legal, because, that is, it proceeds from a source of reference formally competent to enact it. Law exists for what it does; and its rightness is made by the attitude adopted towards it by those whose lives it proposes to shape. Since bodies like the Communist party are in fact an announcement that some lives at least are shaped inadequately by the laws of a regime like our own, suppression seems to me an indefensible way of meeting that announcement. Force is never a reply to argument; and until argument itself seeks force as the expression of its principle, it is only by argument that it can justifiably be countered.

6

I turn to a very different phase of the subject. In every society there are modes of conduct which, though not in themselves harmful, offer an easy prospect of becoming so. It is therefore assumed by many that it is the business of the state actively to discourage such conduct, even to the point, if necessary, of making its most innocuous expression illegal. No one is harmed, for instance, by a moderate indulgence in alcoholic liquor; but since drunkenness is harmful to both the individual and society, the state, it is said, is justified in prohibiting the manufacture or sale of alcoholic liquor. The same principle is urged of noxious drugs, of the use of tobacco, of gambling. Sometimes, indeed, the principle is carried to an extreme point and it is said that the state may prohibit any form of conduct, Sunday games, for example, which a majority of the society finds obnoxious. The claim to freedom, it is urged, may be denied in the interest of a view of social good.

I do not find it easy to accept any single principle that is obvious and straightforward as applicable to the very complex problems we encounter in this realm. Neither the fact that a mode of conduct may be harmful in excess, nor the fact that, whether harmful or no, society dislikes it, seems to me in itself a just ground for its suppression by the law. The first case seems to me one for safeguards against excess; care, for instance, may be taken to see to it that liquor is manufactured at a limited strength, is sold only under careful restrictions, and so on. The second case I find it impossible to decide on a general principle; each particular case is judged upon its own merits. I am prepared, for example, to make it illegal to keep a gaming-house; but I am not prepared to legislate against a social game of bridge played for money in a private house. Conduct must be harmful in itself or in the excess in which it touches society before we ought to seek access to the clumsy machinery of the law.

For we cannot suppress all modes of conduct in which excess does harm. In most cases, we have to leave the individual free to judge at what point excess is a fact. Overeating does great harm, but no one would propose legislation against overeating. Many motorists sacrifice their lives to their automobiles, especially in America; but no one would propose legislation against an undue indulgence in motoring. False social standards result from our excessive adulation of film-stars and athletes; but we should obviously be merely foolish if we legislated against the publicity which makes for that excessive adulation. We have always, I think, to study any proposed social prohibition in terms of the object to which it is applied. We have to remember that it always runs the risk of undermining character by a limitation of responsibility. Men are made not by being safeguarded against temptation but by being able to triumph over it. It would be an impossibility to forbid the use of cheques because some people succumb to the habit of embezzlement. There is a clear case for forbidding the sale of noxious drugs like heroin or cocaine except under severe restriction, because it is clear that their consumption in itself is bound to harm the recipient. There is a clear case for insisting that persons, even

if they be passionate Christian Scientists, who are suffering from
an infectious disease like smallpox, shall be isolated until they
are cured; for anyone who goes about with smallpox inflicts direct
and measurable injury on other persons. But unless we can show
that the particular mode of conduct it is proposed to repress must
necessarily destroy the will-power of those who practise it, as is
true of noxious drugs, or directly and unquestionably injures the
rest of society in a measurable way, I think the method of prohibition an unwarranted interference with freedom.

I take this view on three grounds. I believe, first, that it is
socially most important to leave the individual as uninhibited as
possible in forming his own way of life, granted, of course, that he
is adult and mature. To shelter him at every point from experience
which, if carried to excess, may harm him is not only impossible,
but also dangerous. It makes him pass his life under the ægis of a
system of fear-sanctions which, for the most part, he will be quite
unable to sublimate, and the result will be that sense of continuous frustration which is fatal to freedom. I must, in general,
learn my own limitations by experimentation with myself. I cannot pass my life adjusting my conduct to standards and habits
which represent the experiments of other people. For the reasons
which make the results of particular experiments seem to them
convincing, I may in my own case regard as completely invalid. To
insist that their rule of life is to be mine is, normally, to destroy
my personality. It is to compel me to live at the behest of others
even where I can discover no ground for the behest. Most people
would agree that a statute compelling an atheist to go to church
is utterly foolish. His absence does not affect the salvation of any
other person. His presence there does him no good because his
mood is inevitably one of gnawing indignation at being compelled to participate in ceremonies that have no meaning for him.
Either he will invent excuses which enable him to stay away, or he
will adopt an aggressive disbelief which makes him a source of
offence to the faithful. He loses, that is, the habit of truth, on the
one hand, or the capacity to give and take which makes for decent

citizenship, on the other. Both forms of behaviour do real injury to him; neither produces an attitude of conviction. From the angle of character, the only rules of social conduct that work are those that are self-imposed. And these, so far as I know, are the invariable outcome of experiment made by oneself with one's own personality.

My second reason is not less important. The power of law to define modes of social conduct depends very largely upon its ability to command a sentiment of general approval. What it seeks to do must broadly commend itself, on rational grounds, to those over whose lives its principles are to preside. Legislation which does not fulfil this condition is always unsuccessful and always has the result of bringing the idea of law itself into contempt. For where a particular statute is regarded as foolish or obnoxious by a considerable body of persons, they will rejoice in breaking it. Illegal conduct becomes a matter even of pride. It becomes a matter of principle which gives rise to special pleasure and peculiarly satisfies human vanity. No one in London, so far as I know, regards the average policeman as an unwarrantable attack on liberty; but it seems to be the case that thousands of people in New York regarded the prohibition agent in that way. They wore a breach of the law as a badge of courage, like the revolutionary in Tsarist Russia or the suffragette in pre-war England; and the imposition of penalties upon them aroused in them and their friends an angry sense of injustice. Now I think it is an elementary principle of penal psychology that you cannot make a crime of conduct which people do not *a priori* regard as criminal. Popular sentiment approves a law against murder, and you can enforce that law. But popular sentiment, in England at least, would not, in my judgment, approve a law forbidding the manufacture and sale of alcoholic liquor; and its chief result would be to direct the minds of thousands to the problem of ways and means of evading the law. That is a habit which grows upon those who indulge in it. It loosens all the principles of conduct which make for social peace by making us think of the rules under which we live as

unjustifiable and oppressive. It forces social effort quite unduly
and unwisely in one direction. It persuades government to think
out mean and petty expedients to enforce the law in the same
way as its subjects think out mean and petty expedients for
evasion. The spectacle, for instance, of the Supreme Court deciding that the American government is entitled to tap telephone
wires in order to obtain evidence of infraction of the Volstead Act
is not an encouraging one.[16] That way lie corruption and black-
mail, the kinds of habits which, in England, we associate with
names like that of Oliver the spy,[17] in Russia with that of agents-
provocateurs like Azoff. Few things are more detrimental than
such habits to the moral equilibrium of a social order.

Nor must we forget two other effects of attempted enforcement,
both of which are, I think, entirely evil. A government which is
continually flouted in its attempt at administration is bound to
attempt ever greater severity. There will be an extension not only
of the area of offence, but also of the methods of coping with offence
and the punishment to be inflicted where it occurs. The classic
instance of this result is the government of Geneva from the period
of Calvin's dispensation. It does not result in the satisfactory enforcement of the law, but in its wider evasion. Severity on one
side is met by brutality upon another; one might as well be hanged
for a sheep as a lamb. And the disproportion between crime and
punishment which emerges draws the sympathy of the general
population away from the government to the offender. This is,
I suggest, wholly bad for any society. It makes the habits of government generally suspect to the multitude. It creates martyrs unduly
and unwisely. And this has, of course, the consequence that it
becomes ever more impossible to enforce the law. The law's
irrationalism is advertised to the multitude. It becomes inaccept-
able to an ever-increasing circle who, while they may sympathize
with its principle, are not prepared to acquiesce in the price that

---

[16] 277 U.S. 438.
[17] John L. Hammond and Barbara Hammond, *The Skilled Labourer, 1760–
1832* (New York: Longmans, Green and Company, 1919), Chap. XII.

has to be paid for its application. Not only does such legislation perish, sooner or later, but the habits to which it gives rise persist and are frequently carried over into realms where they are still more undesirable. And the severity which a government is tempted to practise makes it blind to wrong through becoming inured to its consequences. When the British government first met the weapon of the hunger strike it was baffled; later it turned that weapon against those who employed it by what was called the Cat and Mouse Act.[18] Much of this proceeding, where the suffragettes were concerned, had a comic as well as a tragic side. But the whole procedure had the serious result of making the public expect that any hunger strike would be a dramatic battle between the government and its prisoner, in which the cause of the imprisonment was lost sight of in the gamble of the procedure. The public, accordingly, was not greatly moved by the hunger strikes which took place during the Irish Revolution; and when Mr. Lloyd George left the Lord Mayor of Cork to die, people were more interested in the circumstances of his death than in the vital question of whether he should have been allowed to die. In all this realm, the denial of liberty seems to result in the slow maximization of unhappiness.

The second effect is also wholly bad. Whenever government interferes to suppress some service which a considerable body of persons think they require, when, also, the suppression is disapproved by a large number of citizens, an industry to supply that service will come into existence. Its ways will be devious, its charges will be high. It will attract to its ranks many of the most undesirable elements in society. It will form an army of lawbreakers whose habits will only too often be condoned by a large section of public opinion. That has been the case with bootleggers in America and with night-clubs in London. And the risks being great, the profits are high; the interests to be protected are consequently correspondingly great. The history of these adventures in England and

[18] Under this statute people who went on hunger strike were, when in danger of death, released, only to be arrested again on their recovery.

America is one of organized immorality and corruption. Condemnation by the law seems to have little or no effect in dispelling their influence. Men and women attain power through this means who normally would be shunned by most decent-minded persons. The degree to which the police are corrupted by these influences is very difficult to exaggerate. There is hardly a bribe too high for the illegal interests to pay. They are organizing, too, an adventure which stimulates every sort of dubious instinct in perfectly ordinary people. Mr. Babbitt approaches his bootlegger, you will remember, in something like a religious frame of mind. The night-club habitué finds nothing quite so exciting as the prospect of a raid; and he leaves his meretricious surroundings with the sense that he knows the glory of danger and has escaped the humdrum pettiness or suburbia. I think it bad for society to make illegal conduct heroic. I think it still worse to make the central figures in the drama of illegality powerful in the lives of those to whom they purvey their service; they are men and women whose methods of obtaining a living it does not occur to their clients to condemn. Nor is it an answer to say that when the law does act, those clients immediately desert the arrested offender, which is proof that they really disapprove. An enforcement which induces cowardice at the critical moment in those who are *participes criminis* does not seem to me anything of which to be proud.

My third reason is rather different in character. Every state contains fussy and pedantic moralists who seek to use its machinery to insist that their habits shall become the official standard of conduct among the population. They are interested in prohibition and uniformity for their own sakes, and every success that they win only spurs them to greater efforts. If they stop the sale of alcohol, they become ardent for the limitation of the right to tobacco. They are anxious to control the publication of books, the production of plays, women's dress, the laws governing sexual life, the use of leisure. They are terrified by what they call immorality, by which they mean behaviour of which they do not happen to approve. They are scandalized by the unconventional; they luxuriate

in its denunciation. They form committees and leagues to prove
the degeneracy of our times. They rush to the legislature to compel
action every time they discover some exceptional incident of
dubious conduct. To themselves, of course, they appear as little
Calvins saving the modern Geneva from the insidious invasion
of the devil. No one, I suppose, can seriously doubt that men like
Mr. Anthony Comstock, founder of New York's Society for the
Suppression of Vice, regard themselves as the saviours of society.
They have an unlimited sense of a divinely appointed mission,
and the whole of their lives are set in its perspective. They are the
men who find in *Candide* the means of corrupting the mind of the
community. They are horrified by the nude in art. They think the
performance of *Mrs. Warren's Profession* the public profanation
of an ideal. They regard Darwin as an "infidel" whose works were
an outrage upon God; and the circumstances of Maxim Gorky's
married life seem to them to demand his public excoriation.

I know nothing more incompatible with the climate of mental
freedom than the interference of such people. They lack altogether
a respect for the dignity of human personality. They are utterly
unable to see that people who live differently think differently and
that in so varied a civilization as ours absolute standards in these
matters are out of place. It is difficult to overestimate the price we
pay for their successes. Certainly no great art and no literature
great in anything save indignation can be produced where they
have sway. There is a reason why from the time of Calvin not a
single work of ultimate literary significance was produced by a
resident of Geneva. It is easy to understand why the grim excesses
of Puritanism produced the luxuriant licence of the Restoration.

These moralists would be, if they could, modern Inquisitors,
without tolerance and without pity, thinking no means unjustified
if only their end can be attained. They are the kind of people who
drove Byron and Shelley into exile, and they remain unable to
see upon whom that exile reflects. Their pride is inordinate; and
human instincts are its chief victim. They are often ignorant,
usually dangerous, and invariably active. Since the friends of

liberty too often sleep, the unceasing vigilance of the moralists not seldom meets with its reward. To me, at least, they commit the ultimate blasphemy, since they seek to fashion man in their own image. I do sincerely plead that, especially in a democratic society, they are grave dangers to freedom, against which we cannot too stringently be upon our guard. Especially, I say, in a democratic society. For there the proportion of men zealous in the service of freedom is likely to be small unless great and dramatic issues are at stake. Tyranny flows easily from the accumulation of petty restrictions. It is important that each should have to prove its undeniable social necessity before it is admitted within the fabric of the law. No conduct should be inhibited unless it can be definitely shown that its practice in a reasonable way can have no other result than to stunt the development of personality. We must, indeed, have safeguards against the deliberate exercise of freedom, whether by a person or by an organized association, consciously to promote religious or racial malice; the suppression, for instance, of Jew-baiting by the British Union of Ex-Servicemen, or of Negro-baiting by men like the late Senator Bilbo or the Ku Klux Klan, seems to me wholly justified; and there is much to be said for severe punishment as a deterrent to these forms of disease. But no opportunity should be offered for the exercise of power unless by its application men are released from trammels of which it is the necessary price of purchase. We ought not to accept the easy gospel that liberty must prove that it is not licence. We ought rather to be critical of every proposal that asks for a surrender of liberty. Its enemies, we must remember, never admit that they are concerned to attack it; they always base their defence of their purpose upon other grounds. But I do not, for myself, serve principles which claim to be just if their result is to make the temple of freedom a prison for the impulses of men.

III. LIBERTY AND SOCIAL POWER

1

LET me remind you of the essence of my argument. I have taken the view that liberty means that there is no restraint upon those conditions which, in modern civilization, are the necessary guarantees of individual happiness. There is no liberty without freedom of speech. There is no liberty if special privilege restricts the franchise to a portion of the community. There is no liberty if a dominant opinion can control the social habits of the rest without persuading the latter that there are reasonable grounds for the control. For, as I have argued, since each man's experience is ultimately unique, he alone can fully appreciate its significance; he can never be free save as he is able to act upon his own private sense of its interpretation. Unfreedom means to him a denial of his experience, a refusal on the part of organized society to recognize what he cannot help taking to be the lesson of his life.

But no man, of course, stands alone. He lives with others and in others. His liberty, therefore, is never absolute, since the conflict of experience means the imposition of certain ways of behaviour upon all of us lest conflict destroy peace. That imposition, broadly speaking, is essential to liberty, since it makes for peace; and peace is the condition of continuity of liberty. The prohibitions that are imposed in a free society, therefore, are an attempt to extract from the experience of society certain principles of action by which, in their own interest, men ought to be bound. We cannot, indeed, say that all the principles a given government imposes are those it ought to impose. We can only say that some principles, by being imposed, are bound up with the very heart of freedom.

That is the paradox of self-government. Certain restraints upon freedom add to a man's happiness. Partly, they save him from the difficulty of going back to first principles for every step he has to take; they summarize for him the past experience of the community. Partly, also, they prevent every opposition of desire from resulting in conflict; they thus assure him of security. In a sense, he is like a traveller who reaches a signpost pointing in many directions. Law helps him by telling him where one road, at least, will lead; and it invites him to assume that its direction is also, or should be, his. Clearly this will not always be the case. For it to be so, the end of the law must be his as well, its experience must not contradict his own. That contradiction, as a rule, means punishment for him, since, at the end of the road he takes, if it is not the path of the law, he will find a policeman waiting for him. We must, that is to say, find ways of maximizing our agreement with the law.

I sought earlier to show that this maximization can take place only when the substance of law is continuously woven from the fabric of a wide consent. Here I propose to inquire into certain essential conditions which determine whether that consent can be obtained. I propose to inquire, in other words, into that weird complex of prejudice, judgment, interest, which we call public opinion, and to seek the terms of its adequate relationship to liberty. For if my argument be valid that a man's citizenship is the contribution of his instructed judgment to the public good, and that right action for him is action upon the basis of that judgment, clearly the factor of instruction is of decisive importance. Instructed judgment is considered and not impulsive, ultimate and not immediate. It is a conclusion arrived at after an attempt to penetrate behind the superficial appearance to what is truth-seeming. It is a decision made after evidence has been collected and weighed, distortion allowed for, prejudice discounted. If, for instance, I am to oppose the state in a matter like military service,

I ought not to do so until I have rigorously examined the facts
upon which I build my principles. And that is true of every aspect
of social activity. The first urgency is assurance that the facts upon
which I base my action are valid.

Now the world of facts which impinges upon each of us is
difficult and complex and enormous. None of us can know all of
that world. A large part of it—it may be in some context a fundamental part—we have to take on trust from other persons.
Obviously, it is of primary importance that the things we take on
trust should correspond with the reality on which alone a right
judgment can be made. My view of the proper peace terms that
should be made with Germany will be one thing if I have learned
from the experience of Hitlerism that no amount of rhetoric
makes barbarism into democracy, if I have come to understand
what Franklin Roosevelt meant by the policy of the "good neighbour." But it will be a different peace if, as it is made, we come
to realize that the outstanding German desire is to be in a position
to revenge itself for its defeat in 1945. My attitude to the national-
ization of mines, whether in Great Britain or elsewhere, will
obviously profoundly depend upon, first, the facts in the mining
industry itself, and second, the facts about the operation of nation-
alization in other fields; and, if they are nationalized, I am bound
to conclude that loyalty to principle depends upon what it shows
itself to be, when it is applied. I cannot, in the vast majority of the
problems I have to decide, make my own inquiries into the facts.
Somewhere, sometime, I have to halt and say, "This man's report,
or this paper's account, is a thing I can trust."

It is because opinion is so vitally dependent upon the truth-
fulness of facts that observers have come more and more to insist
on the connexion between liberty and the news.[1] For a judging
public is unfree if it has to judge not between competing theories
of what an agreed set of facts means, but between competing
distortions of what is, at the outset, unedifying and invented

[1] Cf. Walter Lippmann's excellent analysis in *Liberty and the News* (New
York: Harcourt, Brace and Company, 1920).

mythology. Things like the incident of the *Maine,* the Peking Massacre which never occurred, the Zinoviev letter, make an enormous difference to what Mr. Walter Lippmann has termed the "stereotype" of the environment about which I have to make up my mind. I bring already to its interpretation a mass of pre-conceptions which tend to distort it. If there is prepared for me "evidence" which has been strained through the filter of a special interest, the distortion may become so complete as to make a rational judgment impossible. The English journalist who in-vented the word "dole" has built into the minds of innumerable people of the comfortable classes a picture of the unemployed in England as a mass of work-shy persons, comfortably lazy and anxious at all costs to live parasitically upon the taxpayer; the proven fact that less than a fraction of one per cent really avoids the effort to work is unable to penetrate the miasma of that stereotype. The newspapers which belong to the power trust in America, the subsidized press in Paris before 1939, the journals which had to satisfy Mussolini or suffer suppression, the govern-ment newspapers of Communist Russia, these are all efforts to dictate an environment to the citizen in order that the stereotype he forms may serve some interest their owners, or controllers, are anxious to promote. Men may actually go out to die for purposes in which they profoundly believe, though the cause which, as they judge, embodies those purposes has not, in fact, the remotest connexion with them.

We have, in short, the difficulty that the control of news by special interests may make prisoners of men who believe them-selves to be free. The Englishman who has to form an opinion about a miners' strike is not likely to be "free" in any sense to which meaning can be attached if the facts which he encounters have been specially doctored in order to make it as certain as possible that he conclude in favour of the mine owners. A Chinese who hears that the "Liberal" party in Rumania has won a victory at the polls, an American who is informed that London is governed by Municipal "Reformers," approaches the discovery of the facts with a body of preconceptions, derived from quite alien experience, which will make a true judgment of those facts a very complex matter. During the Hague Conference on reparations in August 1929, the Italian newspapers continued to paint Mr. Snowden as the Shylock withholding from Italy its due share, while the English press was equally unanimous in painting him as the protagonist against a continental effort to make Great Britain the milch-cow of Europe. The Italian, or the Englishman, who wished to obtain a just view of the issues really at stake there would have had to engage in arduous researches into technical material about which he might lack competence and for which he would certainly not easily find leisure.

Let us remember, too, that our stereotype of the contemporary environment is only the last phase, so to speak, of the problem. The psychologists are unanimous in telling us how important for our future are the impressions we gather in our early years. Clearly, from that angle, the things we are taught, the mental habits of those who teach us, are of quite primary urgency. It may make all the difference to the intellectual climate of a people whether, for instance, the history learned by children in schools is wide and generous or parochial and narrow, whether its teachers cultivate the sceptical mind or the positive mind. People who are imprisoned in dogmas in childhood will have an agonizing struggle to escape from their stereotypes, and they may well have been so taught that they either, after effort, succumb, or do not even know that it is necessary to struggle at all. I do not know how to emphasize sufficiently the quite inescapable importance to freedom of the content of the educational process.

Teach a child year in and year out that the American Constitution is the ultimate embodiment of political wisdom, and you increase tenfold the difficulty of rational and necessary amendment by the generation to which that child belongs. Set him under teachers like those of whom Professor Harper tells us that seventy-seven per cent "contended that one should never allow his own experience and reason to lead him in ways that he knows are contrary to the teaching of the Bible," and fifty-one per cent that "our laws should forbid much of the radical criticism that we often hear and read concerning the injustice of our country and government," and the openness of mind upon which reason depends for its victories will be well-nigh unattainable.[2] Only those who realize the importance of education will understand how a Southern audience could go wild with anger over an account, in large outline untrue, of German atrocities, and yet listen with indifference to the description of a lynching in their own community so revolting in its detail as to be unfit almost for transcription. And we must add to the influence of the school in childhood that of the home, the church, the streets, in the terrible certainty that there are few impressions which do not leave their trace.

It is unnecessary, if I may so phrase it, to urge men to live dangerously. To the degree that their happiness depends upon making their decisions conform to the facts, they cannot avoid danger. It is dangerous to leave a child in the hands of teachers who believe that all experience and reason must be abandoned which does not square with that recorded in the partly mythical annals of a primitive Semitic tribe several thousand years ago, or who equate patriotism with a fervid acceptance of the present political system. The adult is endangering his happiness if he believes that truth is what Karl Marx said, or Mussolini told him, or the inferences of Mr. Baldwin which the latter had in turn drawn from material prepared for him by the Research Department of the Conservative Central Office. Happiness depends in part upon being able to approach with an open mind facts which have been prepared by independent persons who have no interest in seeing that they are slanted in some particular way. Anything else imprisons the mind in dogmas which work only so long as that mind does not travel beyond the narrow confines within which the dogmas work. Once it goes beyond, unhappiness is the inevitable outcome.

[2] I take my account from a summary in the *Lantern* (Boston), July 1929.

How are we to get independent fact-finding and the open mind? The answer, of course, is the tragic one that there is no high road to them. Partly, we may get them through the development of particular techniques, but, most largely, through the kind of educational methods we use, and through the purposes for which those methods are employed. I entirely agree that a multiplication of independent fact-finding agencies, as disinterested and impartial about wages and other social conditions as a medical man in the making of a diagnosis, will take us some distance.[3] Not, I think, very far; for between the finding of facts by independent agencies and the driving of them home to the public are interpolated just those factors of special interest which are the enemies we confront. I agree, too, that freedom is rarely better served than when a great public organ falls into the hands of one who, like C. P. Scott with his *Manchester Guardian,* determines to make news and truth coincide. But men like Mr. Scott are rare enough to make reliance upon their emergence a very dubious ground of hope. Nor need we deny that the growth of a professional spirit among journalists, their organization into a profession with standards of entrance and performance, will add greatly to the chances of solving the problem. So, also, will the development of specialized journals of opinion and of new inventions like the wireless. To some extent—not, I think, a great extent—competitive fact-finding makes for truth. Outrageous propaganda tends to kill itself; men begin to doubt the "papers" when they have found them lying at some point where the facts forced themselves upon attention.

And so, too, with a training for the open mind in schools. People may come to see that where the quality of intelligence is concerned, the second-rate, the dull, the incurious, the routine, simply will not do. They may be prepared to make education a profession sufficiently well paid to attract the highest ability, and sufficiently honourable to satisfy the keenest ambition. Even now

3 Walter Lippmann, *Public Opinion* (New York: Harcourt, Brace and Company, 1922).

we cannot overestimate the influence exerted in his generation by a great teacher. Do what we will, let him teach what he please, the minds with which he is in contact will go along with his mind, they will learn his enthusiasms, share his zest in inquiry. It may be Huxley in London, William James at Harvard, Marc Bloch in Paris. Students who have lived with such men are their spiritual children, not less the products of influence than those who have learned the habits of a gentleman at Eton or a proper respect for the Emperor of Japan in Tokyo. And, equally, we may learn that a narrow patriotism in history and politics has social results less admirable than a quick scepticism built from the sense that our country has not always been right, our institutional standards not invariably perfect. Our governors may be willing to admit that one inference from the rebellion of Washington is the possible legitimacy of rebellion, that one inference even from the new theology of Jesus is that we are sometimes justified in the making of new theologies. It is even possible that the value of the power to think may become so much more widely recognized that we shall not ask that those who are able creatively to teach supreme art be dismissed because we dislike either what they teach or the opinions they profess outside the practice of their profession. We may come to insist upon security of tenure for the teacher even when his principles of faith do not coincide with those for which we desire the triumph.

Yet these possibilities do not, in themselves, seem to me to confer a right to optimism if they stand alone. If it pays to spread false news, we may be sure that false news will be spread. If some special interest gains by corrupting the facts, so far as possible the facts will be corrupted. If a poor educational system strengthens the existing foundations of power, it will tend to remain poor; if its extension is costly, those who are to bear the cost will find good reason either not to extend it, or to proceed at such a snail's pace that the new way has no chance of affecting mankind except in terms of geological time. Our difficulty is the twofold one that propaganda can produce immense results in a brief space of time and that creative educational change takes something like a generation before its results are manifest upon a wide scale. The forces at work to prevent the emergence of truth, the forces, also, which have every reason to dislike the development of the mind which seeks for truth, are many and concentrated and powerful. They do not want the general reporting of experience, but only of that experience which favours themselves. They do not want the general population so trained as to prize truth, but only so trained that they believe whatever they read. In our own day it would not be an unfair description of education to define it as the art which teaches men to be deceived by the printed word. Those who profit by that deception are, at the moment, the masters of society.

For we must remember that in these matters we have to concern ourselves with short-term values and not long-term values. We do not legislate for some inconceivable Utopia to be born in some unimaginable time, but for the kind of world we know ourselves, for lives like our own lives. The freedom we ask we have to make. Every postponement we accept, every failure before which we are dumb, only consolidates the forces that are hostile to freedom. They themselves realize this well enough. They have, in the past, fought every step on every road to freedom because they have seen that the accumulation of small concessions will, in the end, be their defeat. Everywhere they have been guilty of definite error or wrong, they have denied the error or wrong, lest it upset faith in their own right to power. Not the least powerful force, you will recollect, which persuaded to silence even those who thought Sacco and Vanzetti innocent, was the fear that proof of that innocence might disturb popular faith in the Massachusetts courts. The same was true in the Dreyfus case. The same, on a lesser plane, was true of Mr. Winston Churchill when he sought to deceive the House of Commons over the treatment of Lady Constance Lytton in prison.[4] Those in power will always

4 Cf. Lady Constance Lytton and Jane Warton, *Prisons and Prisoners* (New York: George H. Doran Company, 1914).

deny freedom if, thereby, they can conceal wrong. And any successful denial makes its repetition easier. Had California released Mooney in 1916, when the world knew he was innocent, it would have been easier for Massachusetts to have acted justly ten years later. The will to freedom, like the will to power, is a habit, and it perishes of atrophy.

The inference I would draw is the quite basic one that in any society men have an equal interest in freedom only when they have an equal interest in its results. Where freedom's benefits are already possessed by some, this portion of the population seldom has the imagination to see the consequences of their denial to others. They will persuade themselves that those others are contented with their lot, or made differently in nature, so that they are unfit to enjoy what others possess. There is no myth we are not capable of inventing to lull our consciences. We see the futility of action on our part, because we are so unimportant. We see that it would be dangerous in this particular case, because we have an influence that, in other cases, might be exerted to useful purpose. We don't think the time has come for action. We think that action here might lead to other and quite unjustifiable demands. We would have associated ourselves with the demand, but those who are making it, or the way in which it is being made, unfortunately render this impossible. Life is so complex and tangled and full that those who desire to abstain from the battle for freedom can always find ample excuse. The workingman may be afraid for his job; Babbitt may shrink from being shunned by the group whose fellowship is his life; it may be the handful of silver, the riband for the coat, the love of power, the loathing of what freedom may bring. Whatever the motive of abstention, let us remember that men think differently who live differently, and that, as they think, so they build principles of action to remedy what, in their lives, they find bitter or unjust, to preserve what they find pleasant or right.

We cannot, of course, remedy all experience which makes for a sense of bitterness or injustice. Things like the betrayal of friendship are, only too often, beyond the power of organization to affect. But the sense of bitterness or injustice that comes from bad housing, low wages, or the denial of an adequate political status, these we are able to remedy by social action. Or, rather, we are free to move to their remedy, if we have an equal interest in doing so. If our interest is unequal, our sense of a need to share with others in action will be small. Other things will seem more significant or more urgent; and the need itself will shrink as they obtrude. The less we live in the experience of our neighbours, the less shall we feel wrong in the denial of their wants. Trade unionists appreciate a demand for higher wages more keenly than employers: the wealthy rentier reads of a strike in the cotton trade as a newspaper incident, of a railway dispute, whatever its grounds, as a threat to the community. The sense of solidarity comes only when the result of joint action impinges equally on the common life.

We are in the difficulty that every step we take towards freedom is a step towards the equalization of privileges now held unequally. Those who hold them are not anxious to abandon what they entail; sometimes they can even persuade themselves that the well-being of society depends upon a refusal to surrender them. For them, therefore, the honest publication of facts, the making of free minds, are simply paths to disaster. Why should they surrender their weapons of defence? Why, the more, when many of them do not even suspect that they fight with poisoned weapons? To explain to a loyal Roman Catholic that he should tell his children that there is grave reason to deny the truth of all he believes is to invite him to shatter the foundation upon which he has built his life. To suggest to the average citizen who took part in the war of 1914 that schoolbooks should abandon the legend that his particular state entered it with the whole-souled motive of serving justice would appear scandalous simply because he is honestly unconscious of any other motive. To urge even upon the public-spirited heir to a great estate the possible duty of acting upon the principle of Mill's argument about the laws of inheritance is, at the best, an adventure in the lesser hope. There was good reason for the unpopularity of the Socratic temper in Athens.

2

I conclude, therefore, that whatever our mechanisms and institutions, liberty can hope to emerge and to be maintained in a society where men are, broadly speaking, equally interested in its emergence and its maintenance. I accept the insight Harrington had when he insisted that the distribution of economic power in a state will control the distribution of political power therein. I think James Madison was right when he argued that property is the only durable source of faction. I think the perception of the early Socialists was entirely justified when they urged that a society divided into a small number of rich, and a large number of poor, persons, would be a society of exploiters and exploited. I cannot believe that, in such an atmosphere, liberty will be a matter of serious concern to the possessors of power.

What will concern them is how they can best maintain their power. They will permit anything save the laying of hands upon the ark of their covenant. They will allow freedom in inessentials; but when the pith of freedom is attack upon their monopoly they will define it as sedition or blasphemy. For if the form of social organization is a pyramid, men are bound to struggle towards its apex. In a society of economic unequals, gross inequalities make conflict inherent in its foundations. The possession of wealth means the possession of so much that makes for a happy life: beautiful physical surroundings, leisure to read and to think, safeguards against the insecurity of the morrow. It is, I think, inevitable that those to whom these things are denied should envy those who possess them. It is inevitable, also, that envy should be the nurse of hate and faction. Those who are denied struggle to attain, those who possess struggle to preserve. Justice becomes the rule of the stronger, liberty the law which the stronger allow. The freedom that the poor desire in a society such as this is the freedom to enjoy the things their rulers enjoy. The heart of freedom, its purpose and its life, is the movement for equality.

And it is equality that is decried by those who rule. It means parting with the exercise of power and all the pleasures that go with its exercise. It means that their wants do not define the ends of production, their standards do not set the objects of consideration, their right to determine the equilibrium of social forces is no longer recognized. Equality, in fact, is a denial of the philosophy of life which is bred into their bones by their way of living. It does not seem to me remarkable that they should fight against this denial. Who of us, on these terms, but would find it difficult to accept as valid experience which contradicts our experiences, a system of value which attempts the transvaluation of our own? Who of us but would not feel that a freedom which seeks radical alteration of the contours of existence is perverse and dangerous and worthy only to be suppressed? The pagan felt that of the Christian, the Catholic of the Protestant, the landowner of the merchant. The new power which seeks its place in the sun is inevitably suspected by the old with whom it claims equal rights.

The equality will be denied, and, with it, the freedom to claim equality. Inevitably, also, the right to freedom will be maintained, and the two powers will, sooner or later, mass their forces for battle. I know no instance in history in which men in possession of power have voluntarily abdicated its privileges. They say that reason and justice prevail; but they mean their reason and their justice. They are prepared to coerce in the hope of success, and they are prepared to die fighting rather than to surrender. It is the result of such a way of life that the ideal of freedom is inapplicable to matters upon which there is urgent difference of opinion between the rulers and their subjects. It is impossible for reason to prevail if men are prepared to fight about the consequences of its victory. And if they are prepared to fight there is no room in the society for freedom, since freedom is incompatible with habits of violence.

Any society, in fact, the fruits of whose economic operations are unequally distributed will be compelled to deny freedom as the law of its being; and the same will be true of any society in process of forcible transition from one way of life to another. Cromwellian England, Revolutionary France, Communist Russia, Fascist Italy, each of these, of set purpose, made an end of the doctrine that freedom was a justifiable object of desire. Or it defined freedom to fit the condition of its own citizens. In each, it was proposed to maintain some particular form of social organization at any cost; to inquire into the cost might result in doubt of the value of the effort; and the value of that freedom which releases reason was therefore denied. A revolutionary state, of course, makes the position peculiarly clear. But the position is not characteristic only of the revolutionary state.

In England, or Germany, there is no freedom where the fundamentals of the society are called into question, if the rulers think that this may cause danger to those fundamentals. The government may decide that William Godwin is innocuous; but it will not hesitate to convict Tom Paine—in truth far less drastic —of high treason. The cause of this attitude is, I think, beyond discussion. If freedom seeks to alter fundamentals, freedom must go; and freedom can hardly help but concentrate on fundamentals in a society distinguished by economic inequality. I do not need to point out the extraordinary timidity of society before subversive discussion of property rights, nor to dwell upon the complicated legal precautions that are taken for its defence. You have only to examine the attitude with which labour combinations are approached by those who possess economic power, as instanced, for example, by the use of the injunction by American judges,[5] to realize that the main purpose of limitations on freedom is to prevent undue encroachments upon the existing inequalities. We announce that we are open to conviction in matters of social arrangement. But we take the most careful steps to see that our convictions are not likely to be overthrown.

[5] Cf. Felix Frankfurter and Nathan Greene, *The Labor Injunction* (New York: The Macmillan Company, 1930), and Charles O. Gregory, *Labor and the Law* (New York: W. W. Norton and Company, 1946).

For the chance that reason will prevail in an unequal society is necessarily small. It is always at a disadvantage compared with interest, for, to the latter, especially in property matters, passion is harnessed, and in the presence of passion people become blind to truth. They see what they want to see, and they select as truth that which serves the purpose they desire to see prevail. The preparation of news for the making of opinion is, indeed, extraordinarily like the old religious controversies in which men hurled text and counter-text at one another. The real problem was one of proportion; but the protagonists altered the proportions that the material might the better serve their cause. Some thirty years ago a Labour delegation returned from Russia with a statement from Peter Kropotkin about the character of the Russian state. A leading capitalist newspaper in London printed all those parts of it which attacked the Russian regime; and the leading Labour newspaper printed those parts of it favourable to the Bolshevik experiment. The readers of the first were, therefore, satisfied with the knowledge that an eminent anarchist heartily disliked bolshevism; and the readers of the second were heartened by discovering that so eminent a friend of freedom was prepared to support a dictatorship as favourable to freedom. You will remember that Luther and Calvin were always prepared to abide by the plain words of Scripture; but each was careful, at critical points, to insist that his own interpretation alone possessed validity. In such an atmosphere, a solution which strikes opposing controversialists as just is not, at least easily, to be found.

This, I suggest, is the kind of environment any plea for freedom must meet in the modern state. Discussion of inessentials can be ample, even luxurious; discussion of essentials will always, where it touches the heart of existing social arrangements, meet with difficulty at least, and probably with attack. Reason will find it extraordinarily hard to organize supporters for its view, if this opposes the will of those in authority. In wartime, any plea for reasonableness is at a discount; and it was at a discount in England during the General Strike, when the government sought at once for the conditions of a belligerent atmosphere. Attack an interest, in a word, and you arouse passion; arouse passion, especially where property is concerned, and the technique of *raison d'état* will sooner or later be invoked. But liberty and *raison d'état* are mutually incompatible for the simple reason that *raison d'état* is a principle which seeks, *a priori*, to exclude rational discussion from the field. It seeks neither truth nor justice, but surrender.

It is a technique, I think, which almost always comes into play when dangerous opinion is challenged by the state. A good instance of this is afforded by the trial of the British Communists in 1925. No one could seriously claim that their effort constituted a serious menace to the state, for they were a handful among millions, and there was not even evidence that their propaganda met with any success. Yet their condemnation was a foregone conclusion, granted the terms of the indictment. And the habits of power were interestingly illustrated by the judge who presided over the trial. He had conducted the case with quite scrupulous fairness, and had shown no leaning to one side or the other until the jury had rendered its verdict. He then made an offer to the defendants that if they would abandon their belief in communism he would adjust the sentence in the light of that abandonment. He made the offer, I do not doubt, in the utmost good faith and in an entirely sincere conviction that Communist opinions are morally wicked. But that attitude was precisely similar to the Roman offer to the early Christians: they could avoid the arena if they would offer but a pinch of incense on the pagan altar. It was precisely similar to the willingness of the Inquisitor to mitigate his sentence where there was confession of heresy and repentance. Mr. Justice Swift seemed to have no realization at all that the defendants were Communists in the light of an experience of social life which, for them, was as vivid and compelling as the Christian revelation to its early adherents; that the offer he made to them was mitigation of punishment in return for the sacrifice of their sincerity; that the state, for him, was Hobbes' "mortal God," at whose altar they must do reverence. His views, of course, were the natural expression of his own experience of life, and, without doubt, sincerely held; but they implied an inability imaginatively to understand alien experience that is pathetic in the limitation it involves. And perhaps the supreme irony in the situation was the fact that to be tried as Communists was, for the defendants, perhaps the highest test to which their faith could be submitted.

When Plato, in the *Laws,* set out a revised version of his ideal polity for application to the real world about him, he surrendered the demand for complete communism which had distinguished his Utopia. But he was still emphatic enough about the need for equality to lay it down that no member of his state should possess property more than four times in amount of that owned by the poorest citizens. The ground of that drastic conclusion was quite clear in his mind. Great economic inequalities are, as he saw, incompatible with a unity of interest in the community. There is no common basis upon which citizens can move to the attainment of kindred ideals. The lives of the few are too remote from the lives of the many for peaceful disagreement about social questions to be possible, if the ultimate organization of the society is not to be changed. The remoteness means that the few will always fear the invasion of their privilege, and the many will envy them its possession. It is not only, as I have said, that men think differently who live differently; it is, essentially, that men think antagonistically who live so differently. That antagonism is bound to result in violence unless the domination of the many by the few is almost complete, or is tempered by so continuous a flow of concession as results, in the end, in the effective mitigation of the inequality. There cannot, in a word, be democratic government without equality; and without democratic government there cannot be freedom.

For the real meaning of democratic government is the equal weighing of individual claims to happiness by social institutions. A society built upon economic inequality cannot attempt that sort of measure. Consciously or unconsciously, it starts from the assumption that there is a greater right in some claims than in others. It cannot be said that response to claims is made in terms of justice. The nature of economic inequality is a compulsion to respond to effective demand, and this pays no regard to science on the one hand, or to need upon the other. It thinks only of the presence of purchasing power and not of its connotation in terms of social purpose. The whole productive scheme is thereby tilted in the favour of those who possess the power to make their wants effective. There is cake for some before there is bread for all. The palace neighbours the slum. And those who find that their wants do not secure attention are, inevitably, tempted to an examination of the moral foundations of society. Their interest drives them to demand its reconstruction in terms of those wants. Liberty means, in such a context, the power continuously to exercise initiative in social reconstruction. The whole ethos which surrounds this effort is that of equality. The search for freedom is for no other end but this.

I do not need to remind you that most observers who have sought to estimate the significance of the democratic movement have seen that equality is essential to it. That was the case with Tocqueville; it was the case with John Stuart Mill; and, in a famous lecture which reads now as though it were the utterance of a prophet,[6] it was the case also with Matthew Arnold. Broadly, their insight converged towards a recognition of three important things. They realized, first, that in any society where power is gravely unequal, the character and intelligence of those at the base is unnaturally depressed. The community loses by this in two ways. The energy and capacity of which it might make use are not released for action; and the concentration of effective power in a few hands means that the wishes, opinions, needs, of the majority do not receive sufficient consideration. An aristocracy, whether of birth or creed or wealth, always suffers from self-sufficiency. It is inaccessible to ideas which originate from without itself. It tends to think them unimportant if they are urged

6 See the lecture on Equality in *Mixed Essays*.

tactfully, and dangerous if they are urged with vigour. It is so accustomed to the idea of its own superiority, that it is resentful of ideas which inquire into the validity of that assumption. It may be generous, charitable, kind; but the surrounding principle of those qualities is always their exercise as of grace and not in justice. An aristocracy, in a word, is the prisoner of its own power, and that the most completely when men begin to question its authority. It does not know how to act wisely at the very moment when wise action is most required.

It is not only that any aristocracy becomes unduly absorbed in the consideration of its own interests. Its depression of the people has the dangerous effect of persuading the latter of its necessary inferiority. The population is unable to carry on its own affairs with order and intelligence. It does not know how to represent its wants with decision. It develops a sense of indignation because its interests are neglected; but it does not know how to attach its indignation to the right objects or, even when it has succeeded in this, how to remedy the ills from which it suffers. An aristocracy, in a word, deprives its subjects of character and responsibility; and, as the revolutions of 1848 so clearly demonstrated, while the people can destroy, they have never been taught how to create. The success of the Puritan Rebellion and the American Revolution was built upon the fact that, in each case, the exercise of power had been a habit of the general population; in the one case in the management of Nonconformist churches, in the other in the governance of local legislatures and town meetings. In each case, a blind government confronted men who knew how to formulate their wants and to organize their attainment. But, in general, aristocracies do not provide their subjects with the opportunity to get this knowledge. Their own effort is substituted for popular effort, their own will for the popular will. The development of the total resources at their disposal is postponed to the preservation of their interest and convenience. They dwarf the masses that they may the better contemplate the stateliness of their own state. But that, in the end, always means that the vital

power of the people is absent at the moment when it is most
required.

The third weakness of aristocracies is their inevitable imper-
manence. There is no method known of confining character and
energy and ability to aristocratic ranks. These, where they emerge
in the people, will always seek the means of their satisfaction.
From this angle, few things are so significant as the history of the
British Labour party. It rose to power largely because there was
no room in the leadership of the historic parties for self-made
men who had not sought success either as lawyers or as business
men. The result was that the knowledge at the disposal of Liberals
and Conservatives, the significant experience upon which they
could draw for the making of their policy, was always narrower
than the area of the problems they had to meet. The lives of the
typical Labour leaders of the second generation, Mr. Keir Hardie,
Mr. Ramsay MacDonald, Mr. Arthur Henderson, invariably
showed a period where the regretful decision had to be taken
against further co-operation with a party which could not see the
needs they saw, which did not desire service to the ideals they
sought to serve.[7] And men such as these make articulate in the
minds of all who have a sense that their interests are neglected not
only the fact of negligence, the demand, therefore, for satisfaction,
but also the search for the principles whereby satisfaction can be
attained. Their insight into a problem to which little attention
had been paid was the reflection of the experience of the class
from which they came, and that experience grew into a movement because those who had permitted the class to be neglected
found that the old battle-cries no longer attracted allegiance
even when they were given new form.

It is curious to note that not even the impact of defeat gives
this lesson its proper perspective to the defeated. English liberalism
has suffered eclipse because, broadly speaking, it was unable to
discover an industrial philosophy suitable to the wants of the new

[7] See for instance, the very interesting letter of Mr. MacDonald to Keir Hardie
in W. Stewart, *J. Keir Hardie* (1921), p. 92.

electorate. It served admirably the requirements of the manufacturer and the shopkeeper who were enfranchised in 1832. It gave
them freedom of trade, liberty of contract, and full religious
toleration. But it never understood either the fact of trade unionism or the philosophy of trade unionism. Its attitude to citizenship
was atomic in character. It saw the community as a government
on the one side, and a mass of discrete individuals on the other.
It assumed that each of these individuals, given liberation from
the special privilege of the *ancien régime,* had the full means of
happiness at his disposal; it accepted, in a word, the principles of
Benthamite radicalism as absolute. But its error was not to see
that the community is not merely a mass of discrete individuals.
Jones is not merely Jones, but also a miner, a railwayman, a cotton
operative, an engineer. As one of these, he has interests to be
jointly promoted and jointly realized. A philosophy of politics
that is to work must find a full place in the state for organized
workers, to whom freedom in the industrial sphere is, in its fullest
implications, as urgent and as imperative as freedom in the
sphere of politics or religion.

The Liberal party did not see this until it was too late. Built
largely on the support of the Nonconformist business man, the
interests it understood were essentially his interests; and to recognize the implications of trade unionism, as Keir Hardie and his
colleagues did, was to invade the interests upon which it was
able to count for allegiance. It was forced, obviously unwillingly,
into concessions like the Trades Disputes Act of 1906; but its
policy, as the detailed history of the process of social legislation
from 1906 to 1914 makes clear, was to mitigate social inequality so
far as it could by recognition of individual claims, and to build
machinery for their satisfaction which continued to neglect the
fact of trade unionism. When, after the war of 1914, the remarkable growth of the Labour party showed how vast was the decline
of the Liberal hold upon the working classes, the Liberal leaders
were driven by the need of self-preservation to the invention of
industrial principles likely to prove attractive to trade unionists.

But these wore the air of being produced for the occasion; and they did not fit into the character of Liberal leadership. For the latter was quite unable to attract to its ranks either working-class candidates or trade-union support; and the emphatic declaration of a Liberal politician that his party could not join the ranks of Labour because the latter was built upon the trade unions showed how unreal was the body of industrial principles which liberalism had developed.[8] It remained an atomic philosophy applicable to a world in which employer and worker confronted each other, as individuals, on equal terms. The assumption was unjustified; and the way lay open for the consolidation by Labour of its growing hold upon the workers. Liberalism remained a middle-class outlook, admirable in its exposition of basic principle, but incapable of adjusting principle to a medium with which its supporters were largely unacquainted.

In an interesting passage [9] Lord Balfour has drawn attention to the fact that the success of the British Constitution in the nineteenth century—it is worth adding, the general success of representative government—was built upon an agreement between parties in the state upon fundamental principles. There was, that is, a kindred outlook upon large issues; and since fighting was confined to matters of comparative detail, men were prepared to let reason have its sway in the realm of conflict. For it is significant that in the one realm where depth of feeling was passionate—Irish home rule—events moved rapidly to the test of the sword; and the settlement made was effected by violence and not by reason. Passion was the essence of the Russian problem. The effort to transform a dull and corrupt autocracy into a quasi-constitutional system came, like the efforts of Louis XVI at reform, too late to affect men who had already passed beyond any possibility of compromise with the idea of monarchical power. The concessions which the autocracy was prepared to offer did not touch

[8] Ramsay Muir in the *Nation*, August 17, 1929.
[9] Preface to the World's Classics edition of Bagehot's *The English Constitution*, p. xxiii.

the fringe of what the opposition regarded as nominal. Nor was that all. Russia after 1917 illustrated admirably the truth of Mill's insistence that "a state which dwarfs its men in order that they may be more docile instruments in its hands, even for beneficial purposes, will find that with small men no great thing can really be accomplished; and that the perfection of machinery to which it has sacrificed everything, will in the end avail it nothing, for want of the vital power which, in order that the machine might work more smoothly, it has preferred to banish." [10]

3

I conclude, therefore, that the factor of consent is not likely effectively to operate in any society where there is a serious inequality of economic condition; and I assume, further, that the absence of such consent is, in the long run, fatal to social peace. I do not deny that men may long postpone their protest against that absence; there are few wrongs to which men do not become habituated by experience; few, therefore, which, after the long passage of time, they cannot be persuaded are inherent in nature. But such habituation is never permanent; sooner or later someone arises, like the child in the fairy-story, to point out that in fact the emperor is naked. If attention is drawn to some need which is widely experienced, the denial that the need is real by those who have not experienced it will not prove effective. Workingmen never found it easy to believe that long hours of work or low wages were the essential conditions of industrial leadership in the nineteenth century. Few Nonconformists sympathized with Burke's attitude to parliamentary reform. Few American trade unionists see in the use of the injunction by the courts a method of preserving social peace in terms of a strict impartiality between capital and labour. Opponents of Mussolini were not moved by his plea that he thought only of the well-being of Italy. Russian

10 *On Liberty* (People's edition), p. 68.

workingmen have probably been often tempted to the view that their Bolshevik masters mistake Communist dogma for social truth.

To satisfy experience, in short, we must weigh experience as we move to the making of decisions. We cannot rule it out because it is not ours; that is the error of autocracy which insists upon the *a priori* rightness of its own experience. We have to regard experience as significant in itself and seek to come to terms with it. If people are mistaken in the inferences they draw from experience, we have to convince them of their error. Our business, hard as it is, is to discover in the experience those needs which must be satisfied if successful government is to be possible. For successful government is simply government which satisfies the largest possible area of demand. It is not mysterious or divine. It is simply a body of men making decisions which, in the long run, live or die by what other men think of them. The validity of the decisions is in that thought, if only because its content is born of what the decisions mean to us. All of us are inescapably citizens, and at some point, therefore, the privacy in which we seek escape from our obligation as citizens will seem unsatisfying. A crisis comes which touches us; a decision is made which contradicts something we happen to have experienced as fundamental; we then judge our rulers by the fact of that denial, and act as we think its terms warrant.

This concept of government, as I think, is the real pathway to an answer to the kind of problem which students of public opinion like Mr. Walter Lippmann have posed. They are right in their analysis of the constituent factors in the problem's making, especially in their emphasis on the difficulties we confront in making public opinion correspond to the realities it must satisfy. They are right, further, I believe, in their emphasis upon the vital connexion between truthful news and liberty; nor do I doubt that some of the remedies they propose would have the vauable effect of increasing the degree of truth in the news. But all of them, I think, miss out on the vital fact that truthful news is dangerous to a society the actual contours of which its presentation might seriously change. It would have been a different war in 1914 or in 1939 without propaganda; the history of political parties would have been different if the principles they announced were measured by their application to total and not to partial experience. It only pays to print the truth when the interest responsible for publication is not prejudiced thereby. My point has been that in an unequal society that prejudice is inevitable.

And that prejudice, in its basic implications, is incompatible with liberty. For what it does is to emphasize some experience at the expense of other experience, to enable one need to make its way while another need remains unknown. The policy of censorship during the war of 1939 meant that everyone anxious for prosecution of the war to the end had ample opportunity to express his view; the pacifist, the Christian, the believer in peace by negotiation, found it much more difficult to speak. Spoken opinion was, too often, taken for actual opinion; and policy, particularly in the making of peace, was built upon the assumption that no other opinion existed save that which made itself heard. To any observer with a grain of common sense, it was obvious that no treaty would be possible of application save as it came from genuine agreement among the victors, and that where, when the glow of war had gone, Germany resisted its application, a public opinion would not easily be found to demand the imposition of penalties—or that public opinion would be divided about their validity. Nothing is more dangerous in the taking of decisions than to assume that because people are silent they have nothing to say.

Yet that is the underlying assumption of much of our social life. We emphasize opinion which satisfies those in power, we discount opinion which runs counter to it; above all we take it for granted that silence and consent are one and the same thing. Every one of these attitudes is a blunder; especially is it a blunder, for which we pay heavily, in matters of social importance. It is extraordinarily dangerous, for example, to assume that

English public opinion disapproved the General Strike because
Mayfair was indignant, the *Morning Post* hysterical, and Viscount
Simon coldly hostile; for Mayfair and the *Morning Post,* even with
Viscount Simon, do not constitute English public opinion. Our
difficulty is that they will be taken to constitute it when it is to the
interest of government so to consider them. Such an equation is
serious, and may well be fatal, to any who think of social peace as
a thing really worth while to preserve.

We must remember, too, what goes along with a process of
this kind. Those who lament the ignorance of public opinion
too often forget that in an unequal society it is necessary to repress
the expression of individuality. Every attempt at such expression
is an attempt at the equalization of social conditions; it is an
attempt to make myself count, an insistence on my claim, an
assertion of my right to be treated as equal in that claim with
other persons. To admit that I ought to have that freedom is to
deny that the inequality upon which society rests is valid. And,
accordingly, every sort of devious method, conscious and unconscious, is adopted to prevent my assertiveness. The most subtle,
perhaps, is the denial of adequate educational facilities; for what
that does in fact is to prevent me from knowing how to formulate my claim effectively, and neglect is the price I have to pay
for my ineffectiveness. My claim, then, however real or just, because it is clumsily presented fails to secure the consideration it
deserves. Or, again, the view of a group may be simply discounted
where that view fails to please the holders of power. Englishmen
were impressed, for instance, when they heard that the government
of Mr. Lloyd George was solid in its determination not to give way
to the miners; they assumed a careful weighing of the facts and a
decision taken in the light of their total significance. But when
they heard that the miners were solidly behind their leaders, they
felt that this was a clear case of ignorant and misguided men being
led to their destruction by agitators enjoying the exercise of power.
The whole machinery of news-making was, as it still is, directed
to the confirmation of that impression; and the chance that the

miners' claim would be considered equally with the government's was destroyed by the weight which unequal economic power attached to the case against that claim. The opinion represented by the miners was not objectively valued. It was the victim of a process of valuation, the purpose of which was to prevent, so far as possible, an alteration of the *status quo;* and this is true of all claims which seek social alteration in a significant degree.

Now it is, I think, unquestionable that in an unequal society the effort of ordinary men to attain the condition we call happiness is hampered at every turn. The power of numbers is sacrificed to the interest of a few. The truth of the facts which might make a just solution is distorted for the benefit of the few. Freedom, therefore, in an unequal society, has no easy task as it seeks realization. For its search is not to realize itself for its own sake, but for what it is able to bring with that realization. We seek religious freedom for the truth our religion embodies. We seek political freedom for the ends that, in the political world, we deem good. We seek economic freedom for the satisfaction brought by making an end of the frustration to our personality, which an irrational subordination implies. Men do not, I believe, resent an environment when they feel that they share adequately in its making and in the end for which it is made. But they are bound to be at least apathetic, and possibly hostile, when the sense is wide and deep that they are no more than its instruments. That is the secret of the profound allegiance trade unionism is able to create. Its members see in its activities the expression of the power for which they are individually searching. Few states—it is surely a significant thing—have ever won from their subjects a loyalty so profound as the Mineworkers' Union of Great Britain, or the trade unions in transport industries. Even the blunders of their leaders meet with a pardon far more generous than would be extended to the political heads of the state. The reason lies in the degree to which the trade union expresses the intimate experience of its members. And until the policy of the state meets that experience with similar profundity, conflict between the government and the trade union will rarely involve the desertion by the members of the association they have themselves made. What the government will represent as disloyalty to the state will seem to trade unionists a service which is freedom.

The point I am seeking to make was summarized with the insight of genius by Disraeli when he spoke of the rich and poor as in fact two nations. From the poor, voluntary organizations evoke the same kind of impassioned loyalty as a nation struggling to be free is able to win from its members. Anyone who reads, for example, the early histories of bodies like the miners' unions, and seeks to measure the meaning of the sacrifices men were willing to make on their behalf, will realize that he is meeting precisely the same kind of temper as that which appeared in the history of the Italian struggle against Austria or of the Balkan fight against Turkish domination. What Keir Hardie did for the miners of Ayrshire, what Sidney Hillman did for the garment workers of America, are as epic and as creative, in their way, as the work of Garibaldi and Masaryk. The latter must have seemed, at Vienna, just as wrong and as unwise as Keir Hardie seemed to the mine owner fifty years ago, or Hillman to the garment manufacturer accustomed, in the classic phrase, to "conduct his own business in his own way." The point in each case is the important one that power is challenged in the interest of self-government; that the focal point of conflict is an inability on the part of those who govern to interpret the experience of their subjects as these read its meaning; with the result, again in each case, that the imposition of an interpretation from without leaves those upon whom it is imposed with the sense that their lives and their happiness are instruments and not ends.

What is the outcome of it all? For me, at least, it is essentially that a society pervaded by the fact of inequality is bound to deny freedom and, therefore, to provoke conflict. Its values are so distorted, its apparatus for magnifying that distortion so complete, that it is blinded to the realities which confront it. We do not need to go far for proof. The daily newspaper, the novel, the poem, all confirm it. Compare Macaulay's glorification of Victorian progress with the picture in Carlyle's *Chartism,* or Dickens' *Hard Times.* Set the resounding complacency of Mr. Gladstone's perorations against the indignant insight of William Morris and Ruskin. Think of the America of President Coolidge's speeches, and the America bitterly described by Mr. Sinclair Lewis. Remember that Treitschke's eulogy of blood and iron is a picture of the same Germany as that which Bebel and Liebknecht sought to overthrow. Guizot's era of the *juste milieu* is the period of Proudhon and Leroux, of Considérant and Louis Blanc, all, their ideas however mistaken, the protagonists of a just society. Men think differently who live differently. If we have a society of unequals, how can we agree about either means or ends? And if this agreement is absent, how can we, at least over a considerable period, hope to move on our way in peace?

An unequal society always lives in fear, and with a sense of impending disaster in its heart.[11] The effect of this atmosphere is clear enough. We have only to examine the history of France after the death of Louis XIV to realize exactly what it implies. Everyone who seeks to penetrate below the surface sees some vast calamity ahead. It may be a visitor like Chesterfield, a timid lawyer like Barbier, an ex-minister like d'Argenson, a philosopher like Voltaire. The government itself, and those with whom it is allied, has a perception that something new is abroad. They fear the novelty and they seek to suppress it, in the belief that a bold front and an adequate severity will stem the tide of critical scepticism. But neither boldness nor severity can stem that tide. The government falters for a moment on the verge of concession. (There was an hour when the ministry of Turgot seemed likely to inaugurate an era of conciliation.) It is too late, because the price of conciliation is the sacrifice of precisely the vested interests with which the government is in partnership. So the *ancien régime* moves relentlessly to its destruction. It is forced, in the hope of salvation, to

[11] Cf. my *Reflections on the Revolution of Our Time* (New York: The Viking Press, 1943), especially Chap. I.

consult those whose experience it has never taken into account; and they find that, if they are to fulfil, they must also destroy.

That is, other things being equal, the inevitable history of such societies. Their mental habits resemble nothing so much as the horrified timidity which persuaded Hobbes to find in despotism the only cure for social disagreement. They are afraid of reason, for this involves an examination into their own prerogative and, at least probably, a denunciation of the title by which it is preserved. They are afraid of concession, because they see in it an admission of the weakness of their case. They magnify scepticism into sedition, and they accuse even their friends who doubt the virtue of severity for betraying the allegiance which is their due. They cannot see that men will not accept the state as the appointed conscience of the nation unless men conceive themselves to possess a full share of its benefits. They minimize the sufferings of others, because they do not have experience of them, and they magnify their own virtues that they may gain confidence in themselves. They distort history and call the distortion patriotism; they repress the expression of grievance and call the repression maintenance of law and order. In such a society, the governors appear to their subjects as dwellers in another world; and communication between the two worlds lacks the vivifying quality of fellowship. For the truth of one party is never sufficiently the truth of another for the members to talk a common language. Every vehemence becomes a threat; and by a kind of mad logic every threat is taken as an act of treason. The society is unbalanced because justice is not its habitation. Even its generosity will be resented because it has not known how to be just.

I do not want to be taken as implying that violence is the inevitable end. I argue only that the irrefutable and inherent logic of a society where the gain of living is not proportioned to toil is one of which violence is the inevitable end. We have never any choice in history except to follow reason wholly or, ultimately, to expect disaster; and as we approach that ultimate, the temper of the society will be what I have described. For the rule of reason in a community means that a special interest must always give way before the principles reason discovers. And the rule of reason is the only kind of rule which can afford the luxury of freedom. That is, I think, because an admission that the claims of reason are paramount makes possible the emergence of a spirit of compromise. The basis of the society being just, men are not prepared for conflict over detail; but when the basis itself is unacceptable, conflict over detail is magnified into a fight over principle. In such a temper, men's discussions always take place on the edge of a precipice. Social discussion becomes Carlyle's ultimate question: "Can I kill thee or canst thou kill me?" Every utterance is necessarily a challenge, and it is suppressed because it will be so taken; every association is a conspiracy and is attacked because it is so imagined. The only way to avoid so poisonous an atmosphere is to be prepared to surrender what you cannot prove it is reasonable to hold. But, human nature being what it is, men do not easily surrender what they have the power to retain; and they will pay the price of conflict if they think they can win. They do not remember that the price of conflict is the destruction of freedom, and that with freedom's loss go the qualities which make the humanity of men.

4

I spoke a little earlier of the sense of national freedom; and this book would be even more incomplete than it is unless I sought to dwell briefly on what such freedom means. Let me take here as my text a sentence from John Stuart Mill which might well stand as the classic expression of one of the outstanding ideals of the nineteenth century. "It is," he wrote, "in general a necessary condition of free institutions that the boundaries of governments should coincide in the main with those of nationalities." I do not need to remind you of the commentary history has written upon that text. In its name were accomplished the unity of Italy and Germany, the break-up of the Turkish, Austrian, and Russian empires, the separation of the Baltic peoples from the domination of Russia. The economic motive apart, no principle has been more fruitful of war than the demand for national freedom. Even yet, the day of its power is far from ended.

Now nationality is a subjective conception that eludes definition in scientific terms. As an Englishman, I can feel in my bones the sense of what English nationality implies; I feel intimately, for instance, the things that enable me to claim Shakespeare or Jane Austen or Dickens as typically English, without being able to put into words the things that make them so. Every factor to which nationality has been traced, race, language, common political allegiance, shows an excessive simplification which betrays scientific exactitude. It is true that nationality is born of a common historic tradition, of achievement and suffering mutually shared; it is true, also, that language and race, and even a common political allegiance, have played their part in its formation. It is obvious that there is something exclusive about nationality, that the members of any given nation have a sense of separateness from other people which gives them a feeling of difference, of uniqueness, which makes domination by others so unpleasant as to result in profound discomfort to a point which may involve, even justly involve, resistance to that domination. But the fact remains that nationality is a psychological phenomenon rather than a juridical principle. It is in the former, not the latter, sphere that we must seek to meet its claims.

Mill's principle, if carried to its logical conclusion, would mean that every nation has a title to statehood. I want you to consider what that implies. The modern state is a sovereign state, and in terms of that title no will can bind its purpose but its own. The legal meaning of sovereignty is omnicompetence. The state may, as it pleases, make peace or war. A sovereign state can erect its own tariffs, restrict its immigration, decide upon the rights of aliens within its borders, without the duty of consulting its neighbours, or paying any attention to principles of justice. States have done all these things. There is no crime they have not been prepared to commit for the defence or the extension of their own power. A different moral code has been applied to their acts from what we insist upon applying to individual acts, and it is, quite definitely, a lower moral code. The history of the nation which becomes a state and insists upon the prerogatives of its statehood is a history incompatible with the conditions upon which the maintenance of peace depends. That exclusive temper which, as I have argued, is the root of nationality means a measurable loss of ethical quality in those international relations which are concerned with questions of power. You have only to remember the acts which, during the Second World War, states attempted against one another amid the applause of their subjects to realize that the recognition of national unity as a state means the destruction of private liberty and the violation of international justice, unless we can find means of setting some limit to the powers of which a nation-state can dispose.

I am particularly concerned with the exercise of those powers on their economic side. The nation-state is expected to protect the activities of its citizens outside its own boundaries. Its prestige becomes associated with its power to act in this way. So Germany supported the Mannesman brothers in Morocco, England the Rothschilds in Egypt, America its citizens in half the countries of South America. Nationalism becomes imperialism, and this means the enslavement of lesser nations to the imperialistic power. In its worst temper, its eternal character was described by Thucydides in that passage where he relates the tragic end of Melos, a passage it would be mere insolence either to summarize or to praise. Even where imperialism has resulted in measurable benefit to the subject people, as with Great Britain in India, or the United States in the Philippines, the resultant loss of responsibility and character, which an imposed rule implies, is a heavy price to pay for the efficiency of administration that has been conferred. The noble phrase of Sir Henry Campbell-Bannerman that good government is no substitute for self-government seems to me borne out by every phase of the history of imperialism. It is the imposition of a system of experience upon a people ignorant of the character of that experience, for ends only partially popular, and by methods which neglect unduly the relation of consent to happiness in the process of government. The classic case in my own experience is that of Ireland. I cannot find ground upon which to defend the habits of Great Britain there. But those habits seem to me the inevitable outcome of an assumption that Great Britain was entitled to decide alone the character of her own destiny.[12]

Nationality, in short, must, if it is to be consistent with the needs of civilization, be set in the context that matters of common interest to more than one nation-state cannot be decided by the fiat of one member of the international community. Modern science and modern economic organization have reduced this world to the unity of interdependence: the inference from this condition is, as I think, the supremacy of cosmopolitan need over the national claim. A nation, that is, is not entitled to be the sole judge of its conduct where that conduct, by its subject-matter, implicates others. It must consult with them, compromise with them, find the means of resolving the problem in terms of peace. Every one of us can think of functions that, in the modern world, entail international consequences by their inherent character. We have passed the stage where we can allow a state to fix its own boundaries as it thinks best, without consultation with other states. The same is true of matters like the treatment of racial minorities, the scale of armaments, the making of war and peace. Everyone can see that matters like the control of the traffic in noxious drugs, or the treatment of women and children, or epidemics like cholera and typhus, cannot be settled save as states co-operate upon agreed methods of action. Most people can see, at least in principle, that the same thing applies to labour conditions, to legal questions like the law of bills and notes or the rights of aliens before a municipal

12 One must add, in 1947, that the surrender of power by Great Britain to the Indian peoples is one of the great pages in our history, even surpassing that respect for the neutrality of Eire, from 1939–45, for which so heavy a price in lives was paid.

court or the incorporation of public companies. A historian who surveyed the history of international investment would, I think, not illegitimately conclude that there are principles applicable to its control which can justly regard with indifference the question of the nationality of the investor or the state-power to which, save in cases of default, he is certain to appeal. The importance of the supply of raw materials to international economic life forces us to consider the deliberate rationing of that supply and the maintenance of a stable world price level which thinks first of cosmopolitan need and only after a long interval of national profit. A sane man would, I suggest, conclude that if bodies like the International Rail Syndicate or the Continental Commercial Union in the glass industry find it sensible to transcend national competition by international agreement, *a fortiori* the principle applies to matters of world concern.

I am, of course, only illustrating the problem.[13] The principle which seems to me to emerge is the necessity for world control where the decision is of world concern. The inference from that principle is that the rights of the state are always subject to, and limited by, the necessarily superior rights of the international community. State sovereignty, that is, in the sense in which the nineteenth century used that term, is obsolete and dangerous in a world like our world. It gives an authority to the nation-state which, in the light of the facts, is incompatible with the well-being of the world. It invokes the factor of prestige in realms where it has no legitimate application. It means that problems a wise solution of which is possible only in terms of reason have to find a solution amid circumstances of passion and power which obviate the possibility of justice.[14]

For in the external, as in the internal, sphere of the state, the choice is between the use of reason and conflict. The use of reason is the law of liberty; conflict means the erosion of liberty.

[13] Cf. my *Grammar of Politics*, Chap. XI.
[14] This has, of course, become incomparably more true since the discovery of atomic fission, and since the emergence of the catastrophic unbalance between the productive capacity of the United States and that of the rest of the world.

If states are to conduct their operations always with the knowledge in the background that the price of disagreement is war, the consequences are obvious. The atmosphere of international affairs will be poisoned by fear, and fear will bring with it the system of armaments and alliances which, in 1914 and in 1939, issued naturally and logically in war. That was the price properly paid for a scheme of things which assumed that the legal right of the state was unlimited, and which harnessed to the support of that legality every primitive and barbarous passion by which nationalism can degrade humanity. We need not be afraid to assert that, in the international sphere, the sovereignty of the state simply means the right of any powerful nation to impose its own conception of self-interest on its weaker opponents. It is the old doctrine of self-help clothed in legal form; the doctrine against which law itself came as a protest in the name of order and common sense. And exactly as we cannot admit the right of a man to make his own law in the internal life of the community, so we cannot allow the single nation-state to make its own law in the wider life of the international community. Because that is what the sovereignty of the state ultimately means; it is a conception which outrages the patent needs of international well-being.

I conclude, therefore, that if the nation is entitled to self-government, it is to a self-government limited and defined by the demands of a wider interest. I conclude that its recognition as a state, if sovereignty be involved in that recognition, is incompatible with a just system of international relations. It is, further, incompatible with the notion of an international law regarded as binding upon the member-states of the international community. I need not dwell upon the impossible difficulties in which the defenders of the doctrine of sovereignty have found themselves.[15] In its extreme form it has even led a great jurist to write of

---

[15] Cf. Hersh Lauterpacht, *Private Law Sources and Analogies of International Law* (London: Longmans, Green and Company, 1927), for a brilliant discussion of this question; and my paper "Law and the State" in *Studies in Law and Politics* (New ed., London: 1944).

war as the supreme expression of the national will.[16] I am unable to share such a view. Where war begins, freedom ends. Where war begins, the opportunity of finding just solutions of any problem in dispute is indefinitely postponed. And although under modern conditions a whole nation is implicated in war after its beginning, that is not the case either with its preparation or its declaration. These are affairs of the agents of the state, and their interest in the action they take may be totally at variance with the interest of the people for whom they are taken as acting. They may be serving private ambition or a particular party; they may be acting on false information or wrong conceptions. My point is that they dispose of the whole power of the state and that there is no means of checking their activity save the very unlikely means of revolution. The full implications of national sovereignty are a licence to wreck civilization. I cannot recognize those implications as necessary to a proper view of national freedom.

I deny, therefore, that there is any qualitative difference between the interests or the rights of states and the interests or rights of other associations or individuals. The purposes of states are ordinary human purposes like any others: they are a means to the happiness of their members. States have, it seems to me, to be judged by exactly the same principles as those by which we judge the conduct of a trade union, or a church, or a scientific society. They do not constitute a corporate person living on a plane different from, and having standards other than, those of the individuals of whom they are composed. I fully agree that no decision ought to be taken about them, in the making of which they do not amply share. I fully agree, also, that limitations imposed upon their activities must pay scrupulous regard to the psychological facts out of which they are built. I do not, for instance, deny that the partition of Poland was a crime against Poland, or that its inevitable result was to persuade millions of human beings that a war for their resuscitation was a morally

[16] Erich Kaufmann, *Das Wesen des Völkerrechts* (Tübingen: J. C. B. Mohr, 1911).

justified adventure. But I see no difference between the partition of Poland and, let us say, the suppression in the community of a Communist party. Each seems to me an attack upon a corporate experience—a wrong attack because it does not persuade those who share that experience to abandon its implications. I do not advocate the supremacy of international authority over the national state in order to destroy the national state. I advocate that supremacy as the sole way with which I am acquainted to set the great fact of nationalism in its proper perspective.

My point is, then, that the fact of a nation's existence does not entitle it to the full panoply of a sovereign state. Scotland and Wales are both of them nations; neither possesses that panoply; neither, I think, suffers in moral or psychological stature by reason of its absence. Neither, let me add, do the Scandinavian peoples —perhaps the happiest of modern communities—who are only sovereign states upon the essential condition that they do not exercise their sovereignty. But there is no more humiliation in that position than in the position any government occupies in the context of its own subjects. Power is, by its very nature, an exercise in the conditional mood. Those who exert it can have their way only by making its objects commend themselves, as, also, its methods of pursuing those objects, to those over whom it is exerted. The sovereign king in Parliament could legally disfranchise the working classes in England; practically, we know that he dare not do so. Everyone in England is aware of the grim practical limitations under which parliamentary sovereignty operates; no one, I believe, finds humiliation in limits such as we know.

What is happening to the world is something of the same sort. The Charter of the United Nations is an attempt to limit the unfettered exercise of national sovereign power.

It is a painful and delicate operation; how painful and how delicate the timidity that has been characteristic of the organization's brief history makes hideously manifest. At any point in which the history of the United Nations is examined—elections to the Council, the operation of the trusteeship system, resolution of an international dispute, the establishment of United Nations trusteeship—the statesmen at Lake Success have hesitated to act upon the logic of the world's facts. They have seen great nations confronting them, and they have feared that those nations might, if angered, flout the organization and go their own ways. So the old League fumbled and compromised and evaded until it collapsed. The big states controlled it, and over almost all of its history there fell, darkening it, the shadow of the Second World War.

Yet experience of international government should give us hope rather than despair. It took three centuries to build up the sovereign national state to that amplitude which proclaimed its own disastrous character in 1914 and in 1939; it would be remarkable indeed if a generation full of memories and hates so passionate as those of the last thirty years sufficed to overthrow its authority. We can at least say out of the experience of those thirty years that remarkable incursions into that authority have occurred. We have discovered a great range of social questions the solution of which is not relevant to the national state or to the problems of power which that state first of all considers. We have been able, that is, to define areas of government in which national control is not the obvious technique of operation. We have found, further, that a platform can be constructed at New York the nature of which throws any possible aggressor upon the defensive, and suggests the possible organization against it of the rest of the civilized world. We are trying to find ways of reaching the opinion of citizens in different states over the heads of their governments; of making those citizens demand attention to international recommendations in a way that fifty years ago would have been unthinkable. We have shown—and this, in some ways, is the vital discovery of our time—that men of different nationalities can co-operate in the task of international government in such a way as to sink the pettiness of a narrow outlook in the greatness of the common task.

I know that Arthur Henderson was a great British citizen; but I believe his quality as a British citizen was made complete because he was above all a great citizen of the world.

I do not want to exaggerate the prospects of achievement that lie before us; one blunder in Moscow or Washington might easily destroy every hope we may tentatively cherish. I want merely to note that the idea of a world-state is slowly, painfully, hesitantly, taking shape before our eyes. I want to emphasize the logic of the state in an international community so inescapably interdependent as ours is. I want to draw therefrom the inference that national sovereignty and the international community confront one another as incompatibles. Even the states which are most suspicious of the United Nations are, in a degree to which they are themselves unconscious, within the orbit of that influence which its idea makes so compelling. There is hardly one aspect of the United Nations' activity which does not make the defence of sovereign independence more difficult; and even the Russian insistence upon it is more a safeguard of its special philosophy than a denial of the need to transcend national boundaries.

I believe, accordingly, that we can retain all that is essential to the freedom of national life, and yet fully admit the implications of the international community. We can leave to England, for instance, her full cultural independence, her characteristic internal institutions, her special contacts with the Dominions she has begotten; her sacrifice of the predominance of her navy and of her right, by its means, to dictate the law of the sea, has still left her England. She would still be England even if, to push speculation to the furthest point, the Suez Canal were internationalized and Gibraltar returned to Spain. France would be not the less France if French Indo-China were liberated from exploitation, if she gave up her zeal for a conscript army, if she built her frontiers upon the impalpable solidity of friendship rather than the shifting waters of the Rhine. I can see nothing in the conceivable policy of a stronger international authority which would take from her the glory that has made her the Athens of the

modern world. Changes in legal policy, a different colonial outlook, a willingness to improve the physical standards of labour,
world ownership and control of the sources and manufacture of
atomic energy, an acceptance of naval and military forces determined upon the basis of world safety instead of national aggres-
siveness—it is difficult to see in any of these things such a blow at
freedom as would destroy the prospect of national happiness. I
can see grounds for the view that an international authority which
forbade the teaching of French in French schools, or altered the
boundary of France so as to make Marseilles Italian, or sought
without French initiative the abrogation of the French civil code
with its profound impact on the social customs of France, might
reasonably be regarded as invading what in a nation's life that
nation only can claim to decide. I can see that a nation might feel
an international authority to be oppressive if it sought, say, by a
wholesale policy of fruitless immigration seriously to alter the
mores of a national life; it should not impose Japanese immigration on California any more than Great Britain seeks to impose it
upon Australia. I can even see that oppression might be felt
where, in the building of an international civil service, there was
a sense that there was discrimination against the members of any
particular nation, or where in composing committees of international government, proper attention was not given to the claims of
some particular country.

The likelihood of any of these difficulties becoming real is,
surely, exceedingly small. An international authority must presumably be endowed with an average volume of human common
sense; and it is no more likely than any other authority to invite
disaster. Indeed, it is rather likely to fail to embark upon experiments and decisions it ought to make from an excessively
delicate sense of what some particular nation may feel. International life in the governmental realm is much more likely to be a
regime of example and influence than one of legislative compulsion simply because the penalties of national dissent would strain
too gravely the structure of the authority which sought an unwise

imposition of its will. Here, once more, the situation is very like
that of the internal life of a national state. There is hardly any
association the state could not overthrow if it bent its energies to
the task. But most states are wise enough to realize that victories
of this kind are empty victories, that solutions imposed by force
have consequences invariably too grave to be satisfactory in their
application. Consent has its full place in the international sphere;
and it is a safeguard of national right as creative here as elsewhere.
Indeed, it may reasonably be argued that with the disappearance
of national sovereignty the factor of consent is likely to be far more
effective, far more genuinely related to the realities of the world,
than it is at the present time. For consent between two powers
like, say, America and Nicaragua, or Great Britain and Iraq, has
something in it which partakes of the ironical spirit. It is consent always in the knowledge that refusal to agree will make no
serious difference to the result that occurs. But the surrender of
national sovereignty is the surrender of aggressive power; and
the nation can move on its way the more freely since it knows
that it no longer lives in the shadow of international injustice.

CONCLUSION

EVERY study of freedom is a plea for toleration; and every plea for toleration is a vindication of the rights of reason. The chief danger which always confronts a society is the desire of those who possess power to prohibit ideas and conduct which may disturb them in their possession. They are rarely concerned with the possible virtues of novelty and experiment. They are interested in the preservation of a static society because in such an order their desires are more likely to be fulfilled. Their ideas of right and wrong lie at the service of those desires. The standards they formulate are nothing so much as methods of maintaining an order with which they are satisfied; and those they repress or resent are equally methods of establishing a new order in which different demands would secure fulfilment.

But this is not a static world, and there is no means of making it so. Curiosity, discovery, invention, all of these jeopardize by their nature the foundations of any society to which their results are denied admission. Toleration is therefore not merely desirable in itself, but also politically wise, because no other atmosphere of activity offers the assurance of peaceful adjustment. If power is held by a few, happiness will be confined to a few also. Every novelty will seem a challenge to that confinement; and it will always collect about itself the wills of those who are excluded from a share in society's benefits. For this world is not only dynamic; it is also diverse. The path to happiness is not a single one. Men are not willing to yield the insight of their experience to other men's insight merely because they are commanded to do so. They must be persuaded by reason that one vision of desire is better than another vision, the experience recommended to them must persuade and not enforce, if they are to accept its implications with a sense of contentment.

This is, of course, a counsel of perfection. Men enjoy the exercise of power; no passion has a deeper hold upon human impulse. The willingness to admit the prospect of difference, the courage to see that one's private truth is never commensurate with the whole truth, these are the rarest of human qualities. That is why the friends of liberty are always a minority in every society. That is why, also, the maintenance of liberty is a thing that has to be fought for afresh every day, lest an inert acceptance of some particular imposition make the field of action accessible to a general tyranny. For it is impossible to confine the area in which freedom may be permitted to some special and defined part of conduct. Those who have fought for the right to think freely in theology or the natural sciences are not less certainly the ancestors of political freedom. Without Bruno and Galileo there would have been neither Rousseau nor Voltaire.

Liberty, therefore, cannot help being a courage to resist the demands of power at some point that is deemed decisive; and, because of this, liberty also is an inescapable doctrine of contingent anarchy. It is always a threat to those who operate the engines of authority that prohibition of experience will be denied. It is always an assertion that he who has learned from life some lesson he takes to be truth will seek to live that lesson unless he can be persuaded of its falsehood. Punishment may persuade some to abandon the effort; and others may be driven to conceal their impulse to act upon the view they take. But persecution, however thoroughgoing, will never, over any long period, be able to suppress significant truth. If the principles that are urged by a few correspond to some widespread experience, those who recognize the expression of their experience will inevitably reaffirm it. It has been the historic character of persecution always to degrade the persecutor and to strengthen the persecuted by drawing attention to their claims. The only way to deal with novelty is to understand it, and the only way to deal with grievance is to seek a remedy for the complaint it embodies. To deny novelty and grievance a right of expression is a certain, if, indeed, an ultimate, validation of the truth they contain.

We have, it appears, to learn this anew in each generation. We grant toleration in one part of the field only to deny it in another. We grant it in religion to deny it in politics; we grant it in politics to deny it in economic matters. Each age finds that the incidence of freedom is significant at some special point, and there, once more, the lesson of freedom has to be learned. Each age makes some idol in its own image and sacrifices upon its altar the freedom of those who refuse it worship. Ultimately, that denial is always made upon the same ground: it is insisted that the doctrines or practices attacked are subversive of the civil order. The intolerance may be Catholic, when it insists that a unity of outlook is essential for the preservation of society; or it may be Protestant, when, as with Calvin and the Socinians, it holds that the blasphemous nature of the belief anathematized destroys the reverence upon which society depends. The essence of the persecuting position is always that the persecutor has hold of truth and that he would betray its service by allowing it to be questioned. He is able. accordingly, to indulge in the twofold luxury not only of preserving his own authority, but also of assisting the persons attacked to enter, if they so choose, the way of truth.

When attacks on liberty are political or economic, it is their motive rather than their nature that changes. A political or economic pattern has the same hold upon its votaries as a religion; the enthusiasts of Moscow and of Washington differ only in the object of their worship. An economic system defends itself in just the same way as a political system: the devotees of Marxism in its extreme form have never doubted their right to impose their outlook upon the recalcitrant, even at the cost of blood. In a constitutional state like America the suppression of liberty is called the inhibition of licence; in a dictatorship like Moscow it is termed resistance to the admission of incorrect bourgeois notions. Always the effort is to insist upon an artificial unity the maintenance of which is necessary to the desires of those who hold power. Suppression, doubtless, eases the way of authority, for scepticism is always painful, and to arrive at a conclusion after careful testing of evidence always involves the possibility that authority may have to admit that its conclusions are mistaken.

Yet it may still be maintained with some confidence that the only adequate answer to a principle which claims social recognition is the rational proof that it is untrue. It may even be argued that the world would be a happier world if this were the general theory underlying the activities of society. Civilization is strewn with the wrecks of systems which men at one time held for true; systems, also, in the name of which liberty was denied and pain needlessly inflicted. A scrutiny of history, moreover, makes it plain that the right to liberty will always be challenged where its consequence is the equalization of some privilege which is not generally shared by men. The more consciously, therefore, we can seek that equalization as a desirable object of social effort, the more likely we are to make attacks upon liberty more rare, the evil results of such attacks less frequent. No man's love of justice is strong enough to survive the right to inflict punishment in the name of the creed he professes; and the simplest way to retain his sense of justice is to take away the interest which persuades him of the duty to punish. Scepticism, it may be, is a dissolvent of enthusiasm; but enthusiasm has always been the enemy of freedom. The atmosphere we require, if we are to attain happiness for the multitude, is one in which we have everything to gain by the statement of experience and nothing to lose by the investigation of its convictions. That atmosphere is the condition of liberty, and its quality is light rather than heat. For light permits of argument, and we cannot argue with men who are in a passion. Nothing is so likely to engender passion as the perception that one is called on to sacrifice a privilege. The way of freedom, therefore, is to arrange the pattern of social institutions so that there are no privileges to sacrifice.

This kind of plea for liberty is built, after all, upon the simple consideration that the world is likely to be happier if it refuses to build its institutions upon injustice. And institutions are necessarily unjust if the impression they continually produce in the majority is a feeling of envy and hatred for the results they impose. There is something wrong in a system which, like ours, maintains itself not by the respect and affection it evokes, but by the sanctions to which it can appeal. What is wrong in it is its erection upon the basis of passion and its insistence that reason shall serve what that passion is seeking to protect. So long as that is true of our society, we shall continue to deny the validity of all principles which attack the existing disposition of social forces. Those principles may often be wrong; yet sometimes, at least, they represent the certainties of the future. It is always a hazardous enterprise to suppress belief which claims to be rooted in the experience of men.

For no outlook which has behind it the support of considerable numbers will ever silently acquiesce in its reduction to impotence. It will fight for its right to be heard, whatever the price of the conflict. Here it has been urged that conflict of this kind is usually unnecessary and frequently disastrous. It has been claimed that truth can be established by reason alone; that departure from the way of reason as a method of securing conviction is an indication always of a desire to protect injustice. Where there is respect for reason, there, also, is respect for freedom. And only respect for freedom can give final beauty to men's lives.